Knit your own
own
Farm

First published in the United Kingdom
in 2014 by
Pavilion
1 Gower Street
London
WC1E 6HD

Copyright © Pavilion Books Company Ltd 2014
Text and pattern copyright © Sally Muir
and Joanna Osborne 2014

ISBN 978-1-909397-88-0

A CIP catalogue record for this book is
available from the British Library.

10 9 8 7 6 5 4 3 2 1

Photography by Holly Jolliffe

Reproduction by Mission Production Ltd,
Hong Kong
Printed and bound by G.Canale & C. S.p.a,
Italy

This book can be ordered direct from the
publisher at www.pavilionbooks.com

For Lucy

Knit your own Farm

Sally Muir & Joanna Osborne

PAVILION

Contents

Introduction

Knit your own Farm is the newest addition to our menagerie of knitted animals. As children we both used to play with Britains Farm Toys, endlessly making and remaking our farmyards – now we can do it all over again with the knitted version.

We have provided a whole smallholding's worth of animals for you to knit, from the very simple and tiny to the large and complicated. We have also designed a range of baby animals to go with their parents so that you can make farmyard families of pigs, sheep, geese and chickens. We hope that you will want to knit yourself a whole flock of sheep, clutch of chickens, farrow of piglets or raffle of turkeys (which is the collective noun, allegedly).

If you want something simple to start off with, we would recommend one of the babies – the piglet, gosling, lamb or chick. The one-colour animals such as the pig, sheep, rabbit, rat, silkie, llama, goat and goose are also simple. Then if you are ready to tackle something more complicated, we would suggest the cat, horse, hen, donkey, sheepdog, cow, calf

and bull, before working up to the more complex Highland cow (not difficult, but a lot of loopy stitch), cockerel (quite a few body parts) and turkey (lots of body parts and a big job to assemble).

As with all our patterns, you can make them your own; in fact, we hope that you do – use larger needles and thicker wool and you will have a larger animal; make them with your own leftover yarns and your own choice of markings and in any colours you'd like. We'd love to see what you do with the patterns, so do send us any photos of your own versions.

As before, these aren't toys and we use pipecleaners to strengthen the legs and make horns etc, so don't give them to children to play with – you could leave the pipecleaners out, but without the pipecleaners it's hard to get the animals to stand up. We do hope that you enjoy knitting these animals and re-creating *The Archers* in the comfort of your own home.

Joanna and Sally

Cow

A most useful animal, the cow is raised for both meat and milk, as well as for leather. In the Hindu religion the cow is considered a sacred beast, a symbol of wealth and strength, and deserving of the same respect as your mother. In India, cows wander the streets of all cities and seem to have priority over the cars and rickshaws; it is a criminal offence to harm a cow. Cows sleep for a mere four hours a day.

Cow

Many different techniques are used to knit the cow, but it's not too difficult.

Measurements

Length: 27cm (10¾in)
Height to top of head: 19cm (7½in)

Materials

- Pair of 3¼mm (US 3) knitting needles
- Double-pointed 3¼mm (US 3) knitting needles (for tail and for holding stitches)
- 15g (½oz) of Rowan Pure Wool DK in Black 004 (bl)
- 30g (1¼oz) of Rowan Pure Wool DK in Snow 012 (sn)
- 5g (⅛oz) of Rowan Pure Wool DK in Dew 057 (de)
- 2 pipecleaners for legs
- Crochet hook for tail

Abbreviations

See page 172.
See page 172 for Colour Knitting.
See page 173 for Scarf Fringe Method.
See page 172 for Bobble Method.
See page 172 for I-cord Technique.

Right Back Leg

With bl, cast on 11 sts.
Beg with k row, work 2 rows st st.
Row 3: Inc, k2, k2tog, k1, k2tog, k2, inc. (11 sts)
Cont in sn.
Row 4: Purl.**

Row 5: K3, k2tog, k1, k2tog, k3. (9 sts)
Work 13 rows st st.
Row 19: K2tog, k1, inc, k1, inc, k1, k2tog. (9 sts)
Row 20: Purl.
Row 21: K2tog, k1, inc, k1, inc, k1, k2tog. (9 sts)
Row 22: Purl.
Row 23: K3, inc, k1, inc, k3. (11 sts)
Work 3 rows st st.
Row 27: K4, inc, k1, inc, k4. (13 sts)
Row 28: Purl.
Row 29: K5, inc, k1, inc, k5. (15 sts)
Row 30: Purl.*
Row 31: Cast (bind) off 7 sts, k to end (hold 8 sts on spare needle for Right Side of Body and Head).

Left Back Leg

Work as for Right Back Leg to *.
Row 31: K8, cast (bind) off 7 sts (hold 8 sts on spare needle for Left Side of Body and Head).

Right Front Leg

Work as for Right Back Leg to **.
Row 5: Inc, k2, k2tog, k1, k2tog, k2, inc. (11 sts)
Row 6: Inc, p2, p2tog, p1, p2tog, p2, inc. (11 sts)
Row 7: K2tog, k7, k2tog. (9 sts)
Work 7 rows st st.
Row 15: K2tog, k5, k2tog. (7 sts)
Work 3 rows st st.
Row 19: Inc, k5, inc. (9 sts)
Row 20: Purl.
Row 21: K3, inc, k1, inc, k3. (11 sts)
Row 22: Purl.
Row 23: Inc, k9, inc. (13 sts)
Row 24: Purl.***
Row 25: Cast (bind) off 6 sts, k to end (hold 7 sts on spare needle for Right Side of Body and Head).

Udders

Light stuffing is needed for the udders to make them hang down. Tweak the bobbles so that they protrude outwards for teats.

Left Front Leg

Work as for Right Front Leg to ***.
Row 25: K7, cast (bind) off 6 sts (hold 7 sts on spare needle for Left Side of Body and Head).

Right Side of Body and Head

With sn, cast on 2 sts.
Row 1: Knit.
Row 2: [Inc] twice. (4 sts)
Row 3: Inc, k2, inc. (6 sts)
Row 4: Purl.
Row 5: Inc, k5, with RS facing k7 from spare needle of Right Front Leg, cast on 12 sts. (26 sts)
Row 6: Purl.
Row 7: Inc, k13, inc, k7, inc, k3, cast on 3 sts. (32 sts)
Row 8: Purl.
Row 9: K32, cast on 2 sts. (34 sts)
Row 10: Purl.
Row 11: Inc, k15, inc, k7, inc, k7, inc, k1, cast on 3 sts, with RS facing k8 from spare needle of Right Back Leg, cast on 2 sts. (51 sts)
Row 12: Purl.
Join in bl.
Row 13: K19sn, k3bl, k29sn.
Row 14: P28sn, p4bl, p19sn.
Row 15: K17sn, incsn, k5bl, k4sn, incsn, k8sn, incsn, k14sn. (54 sts)
Row 16: P29sn, p6bl, p19sn.
Row 17: Incsn, k16sn, k8bl, k4sn, k3bl, k22sn. (55 sts)
Row 18: P21sn, p6bl, p2sn, p8bl, p18sn.
Row 19: K18sn, k16bl, k21sn.
Row 20: P20sn, p18bl, p17sn.
Row 21: K17sn, k18bl, k20sn.
Row 22: P21sn, p16bl, p12sn, p2bl, p4sn.
Row 23: Incsn, k2sn, k4bl, k11sn, k16bl, k21sn. (56 sts)
Row 24: P3bl, p19sn, p14bl, p11sn, p6bl, p3sn.
Row 25: K3sn, k7bl, k8sn, k2togsn, k10bl, k2togbl, k2bl, k2sn, k1bl, k3sn, k2togsn, k5sn, k2bl, k3sn, k4bl. (53 sts)
Row 26: P5bl, p1sn, p4bl, p7sn, p3bl, p1sn, p13bl, p8sn, p8bl, p3sn, cast on 11 sts sn. (64 sts)
Row 27: K14sn, k10bl, k4sn, k19bl, k7sn, k10bl.
Row 28: P10bl, p8sn, p19bl, p3sn, p9bl, p11sn, [incsn] twice, p1sn, incsn. (67 sts)
Row 29: K2sn, incsn, k1sn, incsn, k12sn, k11bl, k2sn, k2bl, k2togbl, k8bl, k2togbl, k4bl, k4sn, k2togsn, k4sn, k9bl. (66 sts)
Row 30: P8bl, p11sn, p14bl, p3sn, p11bl, p19sn.
Row 31: K18sn, k11bl, k5sn, k12bl, k13sn, k7bl.
Row 32: P6bl, p15sn, p11bl, p5sn, p12bl, p17sn.
Row 33: K1sn, k2togsn, k1sn, k2togsn, k10sn, k13bl, k4sn, k1bl, k2togbl, k7bl, k2togbl, k6sn, k2togsn, k6sn, k5bl, k2togbl. (60 sts)
Row 34: P2togbl, p7bl, p9sn, p11bl, p4sn, p16bl, p4sn, [p2togsn] twice, p1sn, p2togsn. (56 sts)
Row 35: K2togsn, k5sn, k18bl, k5sn, k9bl, k8sn, k7bl, k2togbl. (54 sts)
Row 36: Cast (bind) off 8 sts bl, 8 sts sn, 9 sts bl, 5 sts sn, 5 sts bl, then p13bl icos, p4sn, p2togsn. (18 sts)
Row 37: K2togsn, k4sn, k10bl, k2togbl. (16 sts)
Row 38: Cast (bind) off 2 sts bl, p9bl icos, p3sn, p2togsn. (13 sts)
Row 39: K4sn, k7bl, k2togbl. (12 sts)
Row 40: P2togbl, p5bl, p3sn, p2togsn. (10 sts)
Row 41: K4sn, k4bl, k2togbl. (9 sts)
Row 42: Cast (bind) off 2 sts bl, p3bl icos, p2sn, p2togsn. (6 sts)
Row 43: K3sn, k1bl, k2togbl. (5 sts)
Row 44: Cast (bind) off 2 sts bl, p1sn icos, p2togsn. (2 sts)
Cast (bind) off.

Left Side of Body and Head

With sn, cast on 2 sts.
Row 1: Purl.
Row 2: [Inc] twice. (4 sts)
Row 3: Inc, p2, inc. (6 sts)
Row 4: Knit.
Row 5: Inc, p5, with WS facing p7 from spare needle of Left Front Leg, cast on 12 sts. (26 sts)
Row 6: Knit.
Row 7: Inc, p13, inc, p7, inc, p3, cast on 3 sts. (32 sts)
Row 8: Knit.
Row 9: P32, cast on 2 sts. (34 sts)
Row 10: Knit.
Row 11: Inc, p15, inc, p7, inc, p7, inc, p1, cast on 3 sts, with WS facing p8 from spare needle of Left Back Leg, cast on 2 sts. (51 sts)
Row 12: Knit.
Join in bl.
Row 13: P19sn, p3bl, p29sn.
Row 14: K28sn, k4bl, k19sn.
Row 15: P17sn, incsn, p5bl, p4sn, incsn, p8sn, incsn, p14sn. (54 sts)
Row 16: K29sn, k6bl, k19sn.
Row 17: Incsn, p16sn, p8bl, p4sn, p3bl, p22sn. (55 sts)
Row 18: K21sn, k6bl, k2sn, k8bl, k18sn.
Row 19: P18sn, p16bl, p21sn.
Row 20: K20sn, k18bl, k17sn.
Row 21: P17sn, p18bl, p20sn.
Row 22: K21sn, k16bl, k12sn, k2bl, k4sn.
Row 23: Incsn, p2sn, p4bl, p11sn, p16bl, p21sn. (56 sts)
Row 24: K3bl, k19sn, k14bl, k11sn, k6bl, k3sn.
Row 25: P3sn, p7bl, p8sn, p2togsn, p10bl, p2togbl, p2bl, p2sn, p1bl, p3sn, p2togsn, p5sn, p2bl, p3sn, p4bl. (53 sts)
Row 26: K5bl, k1sn, k4bl, k7sn, k3bl, k1sn, k13bl, k8sn, k8bl, k3sn, cast on 11 sts sn. (64 sts)
Row 27: P14sn, p10bl, p4sn, p19bl, p7sn, p10bl.

Row 28: K10bl, k8sn, k19bl, k3sn, k9bl, k11sn, [incsn] twice, k1sn, incsn. (67 sts)
Row 29: P2sn, incsn, p1sn, incsn, p12sn, p11bl, p2sn, p2bl, p2togbl, p8bl, p2togbl, p4bl, p4sn, p2togsn, p4sn, p9bl. (66 sts)
Row 30: K8bl, k11sn, k14bl, k3sn, k11bl, k19sn.
Row 31: P18sn, p11bl, p5sn, p12bl, p13sn, p7bl.
Row 32: K6bl, k15sn, k11bl, k5sn, k12bl, k17sn.
Row 33: P1sn, p2togsn, p1sn, p2togsn, p10sn, p13bl, p4sn, p1bl, p2togbl, p7bl, p2togbl, p6sn, p2togsn, p6sn, p5bl, p2togbl. (60 sts)
Row 34: K2togbl, k7bl, k9sn, k11bl, k4sn, k16bl, k4sn, [k2togsn] twice, k1sn, k2togsn. (56 sts)
Row 35: P2togsn, p5sn, p18bl, p5sn, p9bl, p8sn, p7bl, p2togbl. (54 sts)

Row 36: Cast (bind) off 8 sts bl, 8 sts sn, 9 sts bl, 5 sts sn, 5 sts bl, then k13bl icos, k4sn, k2togsn. (18 sts)
Row 37: P2togsn, p4sn, p10bl, p2togbl. (16 sts)
Row 38: Cast (bind) off 2 sts bl, k9bl icos, k3sn, k2togsn. (13 sts)
Row 39: P4sn, p7bl, p2togbl. (12 sts)
Row 40: K2togbl, k5bl, k3sn, k2togsn. (10 sts)
Row 41: P4sn, p4bl, p2togbl. (9 sts)
Row 42: Cast (bind) off 2 sts bl, k3bl icos, k2sn, k2togsn. (6 sts)
Row 43: P3sn, p1bl, p2togbl. (5 sts)
Row 44: Cast (bind) off 2 sts bl, k1sn icos, k2togsn. (2 sts)
Cast (bind) off.

Tummy
With de, cast on 2 sts.
Beg with a k row, work 2 rows st st.
Row 3: [Inc] twice. (4 sts)
Row 4: Purl.
Row 5: K1, [inc] twice, k1. (6 sts)
Row 6: Purl.
Row 7: K2, [inc] twice, k2. (8 sts)
Row 8: Purl.
Row 9: K3, [inc] twice, k3. (10 sts)
Row 10: Purl.
Row 11: K4, [inc] twice, k4. (12 sts)
Row 12: Purl.
Row 13: K5, [inc] twice, k5. (14 sts)
Row 14: Purl.
Row 15: K6, [inc] twice, k6. (16 sts)

Head and Neck
Use separate balls of yarn for the black patches and lightly stuff the floppy skin at the front legs.

Row 16: Purl.
Row 17: K7, [inc] twice, k7. (18 sts)
Work 3 rows st st.
Row 21: K6, 3-st bobble, k4, 3-st bobble, k6.
Work 3 rows st st.
Row 25: K2tog, k4, 3-st bobble, k4, 3-st bobble, k4, k2tog. (16 sts)
Row 26: Purl.
Row 27: K2tog, k4, [k2tog] twice, k4, k2tog. (12 sts)
Row 28: Purl.
Cont in sn.
Row 29: K2tog, k2, [k2tog] twice, k2, k2tog. (8 sts)
Row 30: Purl.
Row 31: K2tog, k4, k2tog. (6 sts)
Work 5 rows st st.
Row 37: Inc, k4, inc. (8 sts)
Work 13 rows st st.
Row 51: K2tog, k4, k2tog. (6 sts)
Work 3 rows st st.
Row 55: K2tog, k2, k2tog. (4 sts)
Work 3 rows st st.
Cast (bind) off.

Tail
With double-pointed needles and bl, cast on 5 sts.
Work i-cord as folls:
Knit 14 rows.
Join in sn.
Row 15: K1sn, k3bl, k1sn.
Row 16: K2sn, k1bl, k2sn.
Cont in sn.
Knit 12 rows.
Cast (bind) off.

Ear
(make 2 the same)
With bl, cast on 5 sts.
Knit 5 rows.
Row 6: K2tog, k1, k2tog. (3 sts)
Knit 2 rows.
Row 9: K3tog and fasten off.

To Make Up

SEWING IN ENDS Sew in ends, leaving ends from cast on and cast (bound) off rows for sewing up.

LEGS With WS together and whip stitch, fold each leg in half and sew up legs on RS, starting at hooves.

HEAD AND BODY Sew from front of front legs, around head, along back and 5cm (2in) down bottom.

TUMMY Sew cast on row of tummy (udders) to where you have finished sewing down bottom, and sew cast (bound) off row to front of front legs. Ease and sew tummy to fit body. Leave a 2.5cm (1in) gap between front and back legs on one side.

STUFFING Pipecleaners are used to stiffen the legs and help bend them into shape. Fold a pipecleaner into a U-shape and measure against front two legs. Cut to fit approximately, leaving an extra 2.5cm (1in) at both ends. Fold these ends over to stop the pipecleaner poking out of the hooves. Roll a little stuffing around pipecleaner and slip into body, one end down each front leg. Repeat with second pipecleaner and back legs. Starting at the head, stuff the cow firmly, but do not stuff flap of skin at front legs and udders, then sew up the gap. With de, sew through the udders at the seams from one side to the other to help the udders remain unstuffed. Mould body into shape.

TAIL Attach cast on row of tail to start of bottom. Cut four 5cm (2in) lengths of sn yarn and use crochet hook and Scarf Fringe Method (see page 173) to attach to end of tail, then trim.

EARS Sew cast on row of each ear to top of head, with 6 rows between ears.

EYES With bl, sew 4-loop French knots positioned as in photograph.

NOSE With bl, sew 5 long satin stitches horizontally across tip of nose. With de, sew 3-loop French knots for nostrils.

Calf

Long-legged and wobbly, calves are respectful and dependent on their mothers. An orphaned calf is called a poddy, and a young female calf is called a heifer until she has her own calf. The golden calf is a popular religious idol, mentioned in both the Qur'an and the Bible.

Calf

The calf is easier to knit than the cow. Don't overstuff him as he needs to look vulnerable.

Measurements
Length: 18cm (7in)
Height to top of head: 12cm (4¾in)

Materials
- Pair of 3¼mm (US 3) knitting needles
- Double-pointed 3¼mm (US 3) knitting needles (for tail and for holding stitches)
- 5g (⅛oz) of Rowan Pure Wool DK in Black 004 (bl)
- 15g (½oz) of Rowan Pure Wool DK in Snow 012 (sn)
- 2 pipecleaners for legs

Abbreviations
See page 172.
See page 172 for Colour Knitting.
See page 172 for I-cord Technique.

Right Back Leg
With bl, cast on 9 sts.
Beg with a k row, work 2 rows st st.
Cont in sn.
Row 3: Inc, k1, k2tog, k1, k2tog, k1, inc. (9 sts)
Row 4: Purl.
Row 5: K2, k2tog, k1, k2tog, k2. (7 sts)
Work 9 rows st st.**
Row 15: K2tog, inc, k1, inc, k2tog. (7 sts)
Row 16: Purl.
Row 17: K2tog, inc, k1, inc, k2tog. (7 sts)

Legs
After sewing up, lightly pull the legs to give the calf that gangly, youthful feel.

Row 18: Purl.
Row 19: K2, inc, k1, inc, k2. (9 sts)
Row 20: Purl.
Row 21: K3, inc, k1, inc, k3. (11 sts)
Row 22: Purl.
Row 23: K4, inc, k1, inc, k4. (13 sts)
Row 24: Purl.*
Row 25: Cast (bind) off 6 sts, k to end (hold 7 sts on spare needle for Right Side of Body and Head).

Left Back Leg
Work as Right Back Leg to *.
Row 25: K7, cast (bind) off 6 sts (hold 7 sts on spare needle for Left Side of Body and Head).

Right Front Leg
Work as for Right Back Leg to **.
Row 15: K2, inc, k1, inc, k2. (9 sts)
Work 3 rows st st.
Row 19: Inc, k7, inc. (11 sts)
Row 20: Purl.***
Row 21: Cast (bind) off 5 sts, k to end (hold 6 sts on spare needle for Right Side of Body and Head).

Left Front Leg
Work as for Right Front Leg to ***.
Row 21: K6, cast (bind) off 5 sts (hold 6 sts on spare needle for Left Side of Body and Head).

Right Side of Body and Head
Row 1: With sn, cast on 1 st, with RS facing k6 from spare needle of Right Front Leg, cast on 9 sts. (16 sts)
Row 2: P15, inc. (17 sts)
Row 3: Inc, k16, cast on 3 sts. (21 sts)
Row 4: Purl.
Join in bl.
Row 5: Incsn, k20sn, cast on 2 sts sn, with RS facing k3sn, k3bl, k1sn from spare needle of Right Back Leg, cast on 1 st sn. (32 sts)
Row 6: P1sn, p5bl, p26sn.

Row 7: Incsn, k2sn, k2bl, k21sn, k5bl, k1sn. (33 sts)
Row 8: P1sn, p6bl, p2sn, p3bl, p12sn, p1bl, p2sn, p3bl, p3sn.
Row 9: Incsn, k1sn, k8bl, k10sn, k5bl, k1sn, k7bl. (34 sts)
Row 10: P13bl, p5sn, p1bl, p4sn, p9bl, p2sn, cast on 7 sts sn. (41 sts)
Row 11: Incsn, k8sn, k8bl, k4sn, k2bl, k6sn, k12bl. (42 sts)
Row 12: P11bl, p7sn, p3bl, p4sn, p7bl, p10sn.
Row 13: K11sn, k6bl, k4sn, k3bl, k8sn, k10bl.
Row 14: P11bl, p8sn, p1bl, p4sn, p6bl, p12sn.
Row 15: K2togsn, k10sn, k6bl, k9sn, k13bl, k2togbl. (40 sts)
Row 16: Cast (bind) off 14 sts bl, 9 sts sn, 4 sts bl, p3bl icos, p8sn, p2togsn. (12 sts)
Row 17: K2togsn, k6sn, k2bl, k2togbl. (10 sts)
Row 18: P2togbl, p2bl, p6sn. (9 sts)
Row 19: K2togsn, k2sn, k3bl, k2togbl. (7 sts)
Row 20: P2togbl, p3bl, p2sn. (6 sts)
Row 21: K2togsn, k2bl, k2togbl. (4 sts)
Row 22: [P2togbl] twice. (2 sts)
Cast (bind) off.

Left Side of Body and Head
Row 1: With sn, cast on 1 st, with WS facing p6 from spare needle of Left Front Leg, cast on 9 sts. (16 sts)
Row 2: K15, inc. (17 sts)
Row 3: Inc, p16, cast on 3 sts. (21 sts)
Row 4: Knit.
Join in bl.
Row 5: Incsn, p20sn, cast on 2 sts sn, with WS facing p3sn, p3bl, p1sn from spare needle of Left Back Leg, cast on 1 st sn. (32 sts)
Row 6: K1sn, k5bl, k26sn.
Row 7: Incsn, p2sn, p2bl, p21sn, p5bl, p1sn. (33 sts)

Row 8: K1sn, k6bl, k2sn, k3bl, k12sn, k1bl, k2sn, k3bl, k3sn.
Row 9: Incsn, p1sn, p8bl, p10sn, p5bl, p1sn, p7bl. (34 sts)
Row 10: K13bl, k5sn, k1bl, k4sn, k9bl, k2sn, cast on 7 sts sn. (41 sts)
Row 11: Incsn, p8sn, p8bl, p4sn, p2bl, p6sn, p12bl. (42 sts)
Row 12: K11bl, k7sn, k3bl, k4sn, k7bl, k10sn.
Row 13: P11sn, p6bl, p4sn, p3bl, p8sn, p10bl.

Row 14: K11bl, k8sn, k1bl, k4sn, k6bl, k12sn.
Row 15: P2togsn, p10sn, p6bl, p9sn, p13bl, p2togbl. (40 sts)
Row 16: Cast (bind) off 14 sts bl, 9 sts sn, 4 sts bl, k3bl icos, k8sn, k2togsn. (12 sts)
Row 17: P2togsn, p6sn, p2bl, p2togbl. (10 sts)
Row 18: K2togbl, k2bl, k6sn. (9 sts)
Row 19: P2togsn, p2sn, p3bl, p2togbl. (7 sts)
Row 20: K2togbl, k3bl, k2sn. (6 sts)
Row 21: P2togsn, p2bl, p2togbl. (4 sts)
Row 22: [K2togbl] twice. (2 sts)
Cast (bind) off.

Body

Don't overstuff the calf's body as he needs to look small and young.

Tummy

With sn, cast on 4 sts.
Beg with a k row, work 12 rows st st.
Row 13: K1, [inc] twice, k1. (6 sts)
Work 13 rows st st.
Row 27: K2tog, k2, k2tog. (4 sts)
Work 9 rows st st.
Cast (bind) off.

Tail

With double-pointed needles and bl, cast on 4 sts.
Work i-cord as folls:
Knit 10 rows.
Cont in sn.
Knit 4 rows.
Cast (bind) off.

Ear

(make 2 the same)
With bl, cast on 4 sts.
Knit 4 rows.
Row 5: [K2tog] twice. (2 sts)
Row 6: Knit.
Row 7: K2tog and fasten off.

To Make Up

SEWING IN ENDS Sew in ends, leaving ends from cast on and cast (bound) off rows for sewing up.

LEGS With WS together and whip stitch, fold each leg in half and sew up legs on RS, starting at hooves.

HEAD AND BODY Sew from front of front legs, around head, along back and around bottom.

TUMMY Sew cast on row of tummy to base of calf's bottom (where legs begin), and sew cast (bound) off row to front of front legs. Ease and sew tummy to fit body. Leave a 2.5cm (1in) gap between front and back legs on one side.

STUFFING Pipecleaners are used to stiffen the legs and help bend them into shape. Fold a pipecleaner into a U-shape and measure against front two legs. Cut to fit approximately, leaving an extra 2.5cm (1in) at both ends. Fold these ends over to stop the pipecleaner poking out of the hooves. Roll a little stuffing around pipecleaner and slip into body, one end down each front leg. Repeat with second pipecleaner and back legs. Starting at the head, stuff the calf firmly, then sew up the gap. Mould body into shape.

TAIL Attach cast on row of tail to start of bottom.

EARS Sew cast on row of each ear to top of head, with 4 rows between ears.

EYES With bl, sew 3-loop French knots positioned as in photograph.

NOSE With bl, sew 5 long satin stitches horizontally across tip of nose.

Bull

Often intimidating, the muscular bull can be unpredictable and aggressive: walkers tend to avoid fields with a lone bull. The phrase 'red rag to a bull' is something of a misnomer as bulls are red-green colour blind; in bullfighting it's not the colour but the waving of the matador's cloak that provokes the bull. A copper nose ring is used to control the bull. One of our favourite children's books was *The Story of Ferdinand* by Munro Leaf, about a bull preferring to smell flowers than fight bullfights. In Hinduism a bull named Nandi is worshipped as the vehicle of the god Shiva. The zodiac sign Taurus is a bull.

Bull

A sturdy creature,
the bull needs plenty
of stuffing.

Measurements
Length: 30cm (12in)
Height to top of head: 16cm (6¼in)

Materials
- Pair of 3¼mm (US 3) knitting needles
- Double-pointed 3¼mm (US 3) knitting needles (for tail and for holding stitches)
- 5g (⅛oz) of Rowan Pure Wool DK in Clay 048 (cl)
- 15g (½oz) of Rowan Pure Wool DK in Enamel 013 (en)
- 30g (1¼oz) of Rowan Pure Wool DK in Ox Blood 049 (ox)
- Tiny amount of Rowan Pure Wool DK in Black 004 (bl) for eyes and nose
- 3 pipecleaners for legs and horns
- Jump ring for nose (optional)

Abbreviations
See page 172.
See page 172 for Colour Knitting.
See page 173 for Scarf Fringe Method.
See page 172 for I-cord Technique.

Right Back Leg
With cl, cast on 13 sts.
Beg with k row, work 2 rows st st.
Row 3: Inc, k3, k2tog, k1, k2tog, k3, inc. (13 sts)
Cont in en.
Row 4: Purl.

Row 5: K2tog, k2, k2tog, k1, k2tog, k2, k2tog.* (9 sts)
Work 5 rows st st.**
Join in ox.
Row 11: K7en, k2ox.
Row 12: P2ox, p7en.
Row 13: K6en, k3ox.
Row 14: P3ox, p6en.
Row 15: Incen, k2en, incen, k1en, incen, k2ox, incox. (13 sts)
Row 16: P5ox, p8en.
Row 17: K5en, incen, k1en, incen, k5ox. (15 sts)
Row 18: P6ox, p9en.
Row 19: K6en, incen, k1en, incen, k6ox. (17 sts)
Row 20: P2togox, p5ox, p8en, p2togen. (15 sts)
Row 21: K6en, incen, k1en, incen, k6ox. (17 sts)
Row 22: P7ox, p10en.
Row 23: K7en, incen, k1en, incox, k7ox. (19 sts)
Row 24: P9ox, p10en.
Row 25: Cast (bind) off 9 sts en, k1en icos, k9ox (hold 10 sts on spare needle for Right Side of Body and Head).

Left Back Leg
Work as for Right Back Leg to **.
Join in ox.
Row 11: K2ox, k7en.
Row 12: P7en, p2ox.
Row 13: K3ox, k6en.
Row 14: P6en, p3ox.
Row 15: Incox, k2ox, incen, k1en, incen, k2en, incen. (13 sts)
Row 16: P8en, p5ox.
Row 17: K5ox, incen, k1en, incen, k5en. (15 sts)
Row 18: P9en, p6ox.
Row 19: K6ox, incen, k1en, incen, k6en. (17 sts)
Row 20: P2togen, p8en, p5ox, p2togox.

(15 sts)
Row 21: K6ox, incen, k1en, incen, k6en. (17 sts)
Row 22: P10en, p7ox.
Row 23: K7ox, incen, k1en, incox, k7en. (19 sts)
Row 24: P10en, p9ox.
Row 25: K9ox, k1en, cast (bind) off 9 sts en (hold 10 sts on spare needle for Left Side of Body and Head).

Right Front Leg
Work as for Right Back Leg to *.
Row 6: Purl.
Join in ox.***
Row 7: K6en, k3ox.
Row 8: P4ox, p5en.
Row 9: K4en, k5ox.
Row 10: P6ox, p3en.
Row 11: Incen, k2en, k5ox, incox. (11 sts)
Row 12: P7ox, p4en.
Row 13: K4en, incox, k1ox, incox, k4ox. (13 sts)
Row 14: P9ox, p4en.
Row 15: Incen, k3en, k8ox, incox. (15 sts)
Row 16: P10ox, p5en.
Row 17: K6en, incox, k1ox, incox, k6ox. (17 sts)
Row 18: P11ox, p6en.
Row 19: Cast (bind) off 6 sts en, 2 sts ox, k9ox icos (hold 9 sts on spare needle for Right Side of Body and Head).

Left Front Leg
Work as for Right Front Leg to ***.
Row 7: K3ox, k6en.
Row 8: P5en, p4ox.
Row 9: K5ox, k4en.
Row 10: P3en, p6ox.
Row 11: Incox, k5ox, k2en, incen. (11 sts)
Row 12: P4en, p7ox.
Row 13: K4ox, incox, k1ox, incox, k4en. (13 sts)
Row 14: P4en, p9ox.

Row 15: Incox, k8ox, k3en, incen. (15 sts)
Row 16: P5en, p10ox.
Row 17: K6ox, incox, k1ox, incox, k6en. (17 sts)
Row 18: P6en, p11ox.
Row 19: K9ox, cast (bind) off 2 sts ox, 6 sts en sts (hold 9 sts on spare needle for Left Side of Body and Head).

Right Chin

With en, cast on 2 sts.
Beg with a k row, cont in st st.
Row 1: [Inc] twice. (4 sts)
Work 2 rows st st (hold 4 sts on spare needle for Right Side of Body and Head).

Right Side of Body and Head

With en, cast on 2 sts.
Row 1: Knit.
Row 2: [Inc] twice. (4 sts)
Row 3: Inc, k2, inc. (6 sts)
Row 4: Purl.
Row 5: Inc, k4, inc. (8 sts)
Work 3 rows st st.
Join in ox.
Row 9: Incen, k7en, with RS facing k1en, k8ox from spare needle of Right Front Leg, cast on 5 sts en, 5 sts ox. (28 sts)
Row 10: P6ox, p4en, p10ox, p8en.
Row 11: K7en, k12ox, incen, k1en, k5ox, incox, k1ox, cast on 4 sts ox. (34 sts)
Row 12: P13ox, p2en, p12ox, p3en, p4ox.
Row 13: Incox, k4ox, k2en, k12ox, k1en, k14ox, cast on 3 sts ox. (38 sts)
Row 14: P31ox, p1en, p6ox.
Row 15: K20ox, incox, k7ox, incox, k7ox, incox, k1ox, cast on 3 sts en, with RS facing k1en, k9ox from spare needle of Right Back Leg, cast on 2 sts ox. (56 sts)
Row 16: P12ox, p3en, p41ox.
Row 17: Incox, k41ox, k2en, k12ox. (57 sts)
Row 18: P12ox, p1en, p44ox.
Row 19: K21ox, incox, k8ox, incox, k9ox, incox, k16ox. (60 sts)

Row 20: P59ox, p1en.
Row 21: K2en, k58ox.
Row 22: P57ox, p3en.
Row 23: Incen, k2en, k57ox. (61 sts)
Row 24: P57ox, p4en.
Row 25: K5en, k56ox.
Row 26: P56ox, p5en, p4en from spare needle of Chin, cast on 5 sts en. (70 sts)
Row 27: K16en, k54ox.
Row 28: P54ox, p15en, incen. (71 sts)
Row 29: Incen, k6en, incen, k1en, incen, k7en, k54ox. (74 sts)
Row 30: P55ox, p19en.
Row 31: K19en, k55ox.
Row 32: P56ox, p18en.
Row 33: K2togen, k7en, incen, k3en, incen, k4en, k17ox, k2togox, k9ox, k2togox, k9ox, k2togox, k15ox. (72 sts)
Row 34: P54ox, p18en.
Row 35: Cast (bind) off 3 sts en, k14en icos, k55ox. (69 sts)
Row 36: P55ox, p12en, p2togen. (68 sts)
Row 37: K2togen, k10en, k19ox, k2togox, k8ox, k2togox, k8ox, k2togox, k15ox. (64 sts)
Row 38: P2togox, p51ox, p11en. (63 sts)
Row 39: K2togen, k9en, k18ox, k2togox, k7ox, k2togox, k7ox, k2togox, k12ox, k2togox. (58 sts)
Row 40: Cast (bind) off 31 sts ox, p12ox icos (hold rem 5 sts ox, 10 sts en on spare needle).
Working on 12 sts only:
Row 41: K2togox, k8ox, k2togox. (10 sts)
Row 42: P2togox, p6ox, p2togox. (8 sts)
Row 43: K2togox, k4ox, k2togox. (6 sts)
Cast (bind) off.
Row 44: Rejoin yarn to rem 15 sts, cast (bind) off 4 sts ox, p1ox icos, p10en. (11 sts)
Cont in en.
Row 45: K2tog, k7, k2tog. (9 sts)
Row 46: Purl.
Row 47: Cast (bind) off 2 sts, k5 icos, k2tog. (6 sts)
Row 48: P2tog, p2, p2tog. (4 sts)

Head

Finishing off the bull's head with a nose ring is optional!

Row 49: [K2tog] twice. (2 sts)
Cast (bind) off.

Left Chin

With en, cast on 2 sts.
Beg with a p row, cont in st st.
Row 1: [Inc] twice. (4 sts)
Work 2 rows st st (hold 4 sts on spare needle
for Left Side of Body and Head).

Left Side of Body and Head

With en, cast on 2 sts.
Row 1: Purl.
Row 2: [Inc] twice. (4 sts)
Row 3: Inc, p2, inc. (6 sts)
Row 4: Knit.
Row 5: Inc, p4, inc. (8 sts)
Work 3 rows st st.
Join in ox.
Row 9: Incen, p7en, with WS facing p1en,
p8ox from spare needle of Left Front Leg,
cast on 5 sts en, 5 sts ox. (28 sts)
Row 10: K6ox, k4en, k10ox, k8en.
Row 11: P7en, p12ox, incen, p1en, p5ox,
incox, p1ox, cast on 4 sts ox. (34 sts)
Row 12: K13ox, k2en, k12ox, k3en, k4ox.
Row 13: Incox, p4ox, p2en, p12ox, p1en,
p14ox, cast on 3 sts ox. (38 sts)
Row 14: K31ox, k1en, k6ox.
Row 15: P20ox, incox, p7ox, incox, p7ox,
incox, p1ox, cast on 3 sts en, with WS facing
p1en, p9ox from spare needle of Left Back
Leg, cast on 2 sts ox. (56 sts)
Row 16: K12ox, k3en, k41ox.
Row 17: Incox, p41ox, p2en, p12ox. (57 sts)
Row 18: K12ox, k1en, k44ox.
Row 19: P21ox, incox, p8ox, incox, p9ox,
incox, p16ox. (60 sts)
Row 20: K59ox, k1en.
Row 21: P2en, p58ox.
Row 22: K57ox, k3en.
Row 23: Incen, p2en, p57ox. (61 sts)
Row 24: K57ox, k4en.
Row 25: P5en, p56ox.

Row 26: K56ox, k5en, k4en from spare
needle of Chin, cast on 5 sts en. (70 sts)
Row 27: P16en, p54ox.
Row 28: K54ox, k15en, incen. (71 sts)
Row 29: Incen, p6en, incen, p1en, incen,
p7en, p54ox. (74 sts)
Row 30: K55ox, k19en.
Row 31: P19en, p55ox.
Row 32: K56ox, k18en.
Row 33: P2togen, p7en, incen, p3en, incen,
p4en, p17ox, p2togox, p9ox, p2togox, p9ox,
p2togox, p15ox. (72 sts)
Row 34: K54ox, k18en.
Row 35: Cast (bind) off 3 sts en, p14en icos,
p55ox. (69 sts)
Row 36: K55ox, k12en, k2togen. (68 sts)
Row 37: P2togen, p10en, p19en, p2togox,
p8ox, p2togox, p8ox, p2togox, p5ox. (64 sts)
Row 38: K2togox, k51ox, k11en. (63 sts)
Row 39: P2togen, p9en, p18ox, p2togox,
p7ox, p2togox, p7ox, p2togox, p12ox,
p2togox. (58 sts)
Row 40: Cast (bind) off 31 sts ox, k12en
icos (hold rem 5 sts ox, 10 sts en on spare
needle).
Working on 12 sts only:
Row 41: P2togox, p8ox, p2togox. (10 sts)
Row 42: K2togox, k6ox, k2togox. (8 sts)
Row 43: P2togox, p4ox, p2togox. (6 sts)
Cast (bind) off.
Row 44: Rejoin yarn to rem 15 sts, cast
(bind) off 4 sts ox, k1ox icos, k10en. (11 sts)
Cont in en.
Row 45: P2tog, p7, k2tog. (9 sts)
Row 46: Knit.
Row 47: Cast (bind) off 2 sts, p5 icos, p2tog.
(6 sts)
Row 48: K2tog, k2, k2tog. (4 sts)
Row 49: [P2tog] twice. (2 sts)
Cast (bind) off.

Tummy

With en, cast on 4 sts.
Beg with a k row, work 16 rows st st.

Row 17: K1, [inc] twice, k1. (6 sts)
Work 25 rows st st.
Row 43: K2tog, k2, k2tog. (4 sts)
Work 9 rows st st.
Cast (bind) off.

Tail

With double-pointed needles and ox, cast
on 5 sts.
Work i-cord as folls:
Knit 18 rows.
Join in en.
Row 19: K2ox, k1en, k2ox.
Row 20: K1ox, k3en, k1ox.
Cont in en.
Knit 8 rows.
Cast (bind) off.

Ear

(make 2 the same)
With ox, cast on 5 sts.
Knit 5 rows.
Row 6: K2tog, k1, k2tog. (3 sts)
Knit 2 rows.
Cast (bind) off.

Horn

(make 2 the same)
With cl, cast on 5 sts.
Beg with a k row, work 8 rows st st.
Row 9: K2tog, k1, k2tog. (3 sts)
Work 4 rows st st.
Row 14: P3tog and fasten off.

To Make Up

SEWING IN ENDS Sew in ends, leaving ends
from cast on and cast (bound) off rows for
sewing up.
LEGS With WS together and whip stitch,
fold each leg in half and sew up legs on RS,
starting at hooves.
HEAD AND BODY Sew from front of front
legs, up chest, around head, along back and
down bottom.

TUMMY Sew cast on row of tummy to base of bull's bottom (where legs begin), and sew cast (bound) off row to front of front legs. Ease and sew tummy to fit body. Leave a 2.5cm (1in) gap between front and back legs on one side.

STUFFING Pipecleaners are used to stiffen the legs and help bend them into shape. Fold a pipecleaner into a U-shape and measure against front two legs. Cut to fit approximately, leaving an extra 2.5cm (1in) at both ends. Fold these ends over to stop the pipecleaner poking out of the hooves. Roll a little stuffing around pipecleaner and slip into body, one end down each front leg. Repeat with second pipecleaner and back legs. Starting at the head, stuff the bull firmly, but do not stuff flap of skin at front legs, then sew up the gap. Mould body into shape.

TAIL Attach cast on row of tail to start of bottom. Cut four 5cm (2in) lengths of en yarn and use crochet hook and Scarf Fringe Method (see page 173) to attach to end of tail, then trim.

EARS Sew cast on row of each ear to top of head, with 8 rows between ears.

HORNS Cut two lengths of pipecleaner 2.5cm (1in) longer than horns. Wrap each horn around a pipecleaner so that one end of pipecleaner protrudes and sew up. Push protruding ends of horns into top of head, between and just behind the ears. Sew horns in place and bend into shape.

EYES With bl, sew 4-loop French knots positioned as in photograph.

NOSE With bl, sew 5 long satin stitches horizontally across tip of nose. With cl, sew 3-loop French knots for nostrils. Attach jump ring (optional).

Donkey

A beast of burden and a domesticated working animal for 5,000 years, donkeys still perform important roles in developing countries, despite being notoriously stubborn. Nowadays donkeys are used to carry explosives in wars. Legend relates that the 'cross' marking on the donkey's back and shoulders is a blessing to the donkey from God for stoically carrying Jesus into Jerusalem on Palm Sunday. Famous literary donkeys include Bottom, who dreams the dream in William Shakespeare's *A Midsummer Night's Dream*, and Eeyore, the relentlessly despondent donkey in A. A. Milne's *Winnie-the-Pooh*.

Donkey

The donkey is a
fairly straightforward
knit and a good
introduction to knitting
four-legged animals.

Measurements
Length: 25cm (10in)
Height to top of head: 14cm (5½in)

Materials
- Pair of 3¼mm (US 3) knitting needles
- Double-pointed 3¼mm (US 3) knitting needles (for tail and for holding stitches)
- 5g (⅛oz) of Rowan Pure Wool Worsted in Clove 108 (cv)
- 30g (1¼oz) of Rowan Creative Focus Worsted in Charcoal Heather 00402 (ch)
- 5g (⅛oz) of Rowan Creative Focus Worsted in Moss 00005 (ms)
- 2 pipecleaners for legs
- Crochet hook for mane

Abbreviations
See page 172.
See page 172 for Short Row Patterning.
See page 172 for I-cord Technique.
See page 173 for Scarf Fringe Method.
See page 172 for Wrap and Turn Method.

Right Back Leg
With cv, cast on 9 sts.
Beg with a k row, work 2 rows st st.
Row 3: Inc, k1, k2tog, k1, k2tog, k1, inc. (9 sts)

Cont in ch.
Row 4: Purl.
Row 5: Inc, k1, k2tog, k1, k2tog, k1, inc. (9 sts)
Row 6: Purl.
Row 7: K2, k2tog, k1, k2tog, k2.* (7 sts)
Work 7 rows st st.
Row 15: K2tog, inc, k1, inc, k2tog. (7 sts)
Row 16: Purl.**
Join in ms.
Row 17: K2ms, incch, k1ch, incch, k2ch. (9 sts)
Row 18: P6ch, p3ms.
Row 19: K3ms, incch, k1ch, incch, k3ch. (11 sts)
Row 20: P7ch, p4ms.
Row 21: K4ms, incch, k1ch, incch, k4ch. (13 sts)
Row 22: P8ch, p5ms.
Row 23: K5ms, incch, k1ch, incch, k5ch. (15 sts)
Row 24: P9ch, p6ms.
Row 25: Incms, k5ms, k8ch, incch. (17 sts)
Row 26: P10ch, p7ms.
Row 27: Cast (bind) off 7 sts ms, 1 st ch, k9ch icos (hold 9 sts on spare needle for Right Side of Body).

Left Back Leg
Work as for Right Back Leg to **.
Join in ms.
Row 17: K2ch, incch, k1ch, incch, k2ms. (9 sts)
Row 18: P3ms, p6ch.
Row 19: K3ch, incch, k1ch, incch, k3ms. (11 sts)
Row 20: P4ms, p7ch.
Row 21: K4ch, incch, k1ch, incch, k4ms. (13 sts)
Row 22: P5ms, p8ch.
Row 23: K5ch, incch, k1ch, incch, k5ms. (15 sts)
Row 24: P6ms, p9ch.
Row 25: Incch, k8ch, k5ms, incms. (17 sts)

Legs
When finished, manipulate the back legs to give them a characterful shape.

Row 26: P7ms, p10ch.
Row 27: K9ch, cast (bind) off 1 st ch,
7 sts ms (hold 9 sts on spare needle for
Left Side of Body).

Right Front Leg

Work as for Right Back Leg to *.
Work 5 rows st st.***
Join in ms.
Row 13: K1ms, k6ch.
Row 14: P6ch, p1ms.
Row 15: K2ms, incch, k1ch, incch, k2ch.
(9 sts)
Row 16: P7ch, p2ms.
Row 17: K3ms, k6ch.
Row 18: P6ch, p3ms.
Row 19: K3ms, incch, k1ch, incch, k3ch.
(11 sts)
Row 20: P7ch, p4ms.
Row 21: Cast (bind) off 4 sts ms, 1 st ch,
k6ch icos (hold 6 sts on spare needle for
Right Side of Body).

Left Front Leg

Work as for Right Front Leg to ***.
Join in ms.
Row 13: K6ch, k1ms.
Row 14: P1ms, p6ch.
Row 15: K2ch, incch, k1ch, incch, k2ms.
(9 sts)
Row 16: P2ms, p7ch.
Row 17: K6ch, k3ms.
Row 18: P3ms, p6ch.
Row 19: K3ch, incch, k1ch, incch, k3ms.
(11 sts)
Row 20: P4ms, p7ch.
Row 21: K6ch, cast (bind) off 1 st ch,
4 sts ms (hold 6 sts on spare needle for
Left Side of Body).

Right Side of Body

Row 1: With ch and ms, cast on 1 st ch, with
RS facing k6ch from spare needle of Right
Front Leg, cast on 1 st ch, 8 sts ms. (16 sts)

Row 2: P5ms, p10ch, incch. (17 sts)
Row 3: K12ch, incch, k3ch, incch, cast on
3 sts ch. (22 sts)
Row 4: P3ms, p18ch, incch. (23 sts)
Row 5: K13ch, incch, k5ch, incch, k1ch,
k2ms, cast on 2 sts ms. (27 sts)
Row 6: P3ms, p23ch, incch. (28 sts)
Row 7: Incch, k25ch, k2ms, cast on 2 sts
ms, with RS facing k9ch from spare needle
of Right Back Leg, cast on 2 sts ch. (42 sts)
Cont in ch.
Row 8: P41, inc. (43 sts)
Row 9: Inc, k42. (44 sts)
Row 10: Purl.
Join in cv.
Row 11: Incch, k8ch, k1cv, k33ch, incch.
(46 sts)
Row 12: P35ch, p1cv, p10ch.
Row 13: Incch, k9ch, k1cv, k34ch, incch.
(48 sts)
Row 14: P36ch, p1cv, p11ch.
Row 15: Incch, k9ch, k2cv, k7ch, k2togch,
k5, k2togch, k20ch. (47 sts)
Row 16: P34ch, p2cv, p11ch.
Row 17: Incch, k10ch, k2cv, k7ch, k2togch,
k5ch, k2togch, k12ch, k2togch, k2ch,
k2togch. (44 sts)
Row 18: P2togch, p28ch, p2cv, p12ch.
(43 sts)
Row 19: Incch, k11ch, k2cv, k23ch, k2togch,
k2ch, k2togch. (42 sts)
Row 20: Cast (bind) off 28 sts ch, 1 st cv,
p13ch icos (hold 13 sts on spare needle for
Neck and Head).

Left Side of Body

Row 1: With ch and ms, cast on 1 st ch, with
WS facing p6ch from spare needle of Left
Front Leg, cast on 1 st ch, 8 sts ms. (16 sts)
Row 2: K5ms, k10ch, incch. (17 sts)
Row 3: P12ch, incch, p3ch, incch, cast on
3 sts ms. (22 sts)
Row 4: K3ms, k18ch, incch. (23 sts)
Row 5: P13ch, incch, p5ch, incch, p1ch,

k2ms, cast on 2 sts ms. (27 sts)
Row 6: K3ms, k23ch, incch. (28 sts)
Row 7: Incch, p25ch, p2ms, cast on 2 sts
ms, with WS facing p9ch from Left Back Leg,
cast on 2 sts ch. (42 sts)
Cont in ch.
Row 8: K41, inc. (43 sts)
Row 9: Inc, p42. (44 sts)
Row 10: Knit.
Join in cv.
Row 11: Incch, p8ch, p1cv, p33ch, incch.
(46 sts)
Row 12: K35ch, k1cv, k10ch.
Row 13: Incch, p9ch, p1cv, p34ch, incch.
(48 sts)
Row 14: K36ch, k1cv, k11ch.
Row 15: Incch, p9ch, p2cv, p7ch, p2togch,
p5, p2togch, p20ch. (47 sts)
Row 16: K34ch, k2cv, k11ch.
Row 17: Incch, p10ch, p2cv, p7ch, p2togch,
p5ch, p2togch, p12ch, p2togch, p2ch,
p2togch. (44 sts)
Row 18: K2togch, k28ch, k2cv, k12ch.
(43 sts)
Row 19: Incch, p11ch, p2cv, p23ch, p2togch,
p2ch, p2togch. (42 sts)
Row 20: Cast (bind) off 28 sts ch, 1 st cv,
k13ch icos (hold 13 sts on spare needle for
Neck and Head).

Neck and Head

Row 1: With ch, cast on 1 st ch, with RS
facing k11, k2tog from spare needle of Right
Side of Body, then k2tog, k10, inc from spare
needle of Left Side of Body. (26 sts)
Row 2: P11, [p2tog] twice, p11. (24 sts)
Row 3: K10, [k2tog] twice, k9, w&t (leave 1 st
on left-hand needle unworked).
Row 4: P20, w&t.
Row 5: K8, [k2tog] twice, k7, w&t.
Row 6: P16, w&t.
Row 7: K15, w&t.
Row 8: P14, w&t.
Row 9: K5, [k2tog] twice, k4, w&t.

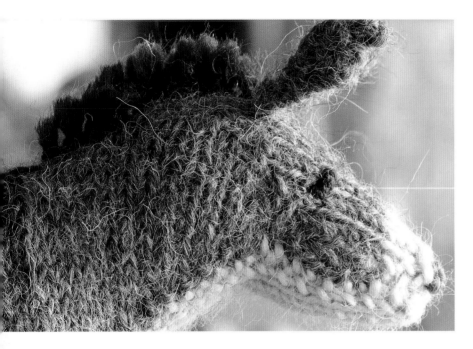

Mane

The mane is made from tassels; you can cut them as long or as short as you like.

Row 10: P10, w&t.
Row 11: K3, [k2tog] twice, k2, w&t.
Row 12: P6, w&t.
Row 13: K7, w&t.
Row 14: P8, w&t.
Row 15: K9, w&t.
Row 16: P10, w&t.
Row 17: K11, w&t.
Row 18: P12, w&t.
Row 19: K4, [k2tog] twice, k5, w&t.
Row 20: P12, w&t.
Row 21: K13. (14 sts in total)
Row 22: Inc, p2, p2tog, p4, p2tog, p2, inc. (14 sts)
Row 23: Knit.
Row 24: P4, p2tog, p2, p2tog, p4. (12 sts)

Row 25: Knit.
Row 26: Purl.
Row 27: K2tog, k8, k2tog. (10 sts)
Cont in ms.
Work 3 rows st st.
Row 31: Cast (bind) off 3 sts, k to end. (7 sts)
Row 32: Cast (bind) off 3 sts, p to end. (4 sts)
Work 2 rows st st.
Cast (bind) off.

Tummy

With ms, cast on 4 sts.
Beg with a k row, work 12 rows st st.
Row 13: K1, [inc] twice, k1. (6 sts)
Work 3 rows st st.
Row 17: K1, inc, k2, inc, k1. (8 sts)
Work 19 rows st st.
Row 37: K1, k2tog, k2, k2tog, k1. (6 sts)
Work 3 rows st st.
Row 41: K1, [k2tog] twice, k1. (4 sts)
Work 43 rows st st.
Cast (bind) off.

Tail

With double-pointed needles and ch, cast on 5 sts.
Work i-cord as folls:
Knit 16 rows.
Row 17: K2tog, k1, k2tog. (3 sts)
Knit 3 rows.
Cast (bind) off.

Ear

(make 2 the same)
With ch, cast on 4 sts.
Knit 10 rows.
Row 11: [K2tog] twice. (2 sts)
Knit 2 rows.
Row 14: K2tog and fasten off.

To Make Up

SEWING IN ENDS Sew in ends, leaving ends from cast on and cast (bound) off rows for sewing up.

LEGS With WS together and whip stitch, fold each leg in half and sew up legs on RS, starting at hooves.

BODY Sew along back of donkey and around bottom.

NOSE Sew centre section of nose to sides of nose, to make a square shape.

TUMMY Sew cast on row of tummy to base of donkey's bottom (where legs begin), and sew cast (bound) off row to nose. Ease and sew tummy to fit body. Leave a 2.5cm (1in) gap between front and back legs on one side.

STUFFING Pipecleaners are used to stiffen the legs and help bend them into shape. Fold a pipecleaner into a U-shape and measure against front two legs. Cut to fit approximately, leaving an extra 2.5cm (1in) at both ends. Fold these ends over to stop the pipecleaner poking out of the hooves. Roll a little stuffing around pipecleaner and slip into body, one end down each front leg. Repeat with second pipecleaner and back legs. Starting at the head, stuff the donkey firmly, then sew up the gap. Mould body into shape.

TAIL Attach cast on row of tail to start of bottom. Cut four 5cm (2in) lengths of cv yarn and use crochet hook and Scarf Fringe Method (see page 173) to attach to end of tail, then trim.

EARS Sew cast on row of each ear to top of head, with 4 sts between ears.

EYES With bl, sew 3 slanting satin stitches positioned as in photograph.

MANE Cut approx fifteen 5cm (2in) lengths of cv yarn and use crochet hook and Scarf Fringe Method (see page 173) to attach single-strand tassels along centre back of neck and between ears. Trim to shape as in photograph.

NOSE With ch, sew 3-loop French knots for nostrils.

Farm Cat

The feral farm cat is a handy pest control expert.
Farm cats live outdoors in farmyards, eating rats
and small animals before the rodents can eat grain
stocks. It's a dangerous life – they are often eaten
as prey by other animals, so for protection some
farm cats sleep indoors, hopefully by an Aga in a
farmer's kitchen.

Farm Cat

Our farm cat is quite porky, but you can make him sleeker with less stuffing.

Measurements
Length: 16cm (6¼in)
Height to top of head: 10cm (4in)

Materials
- Pair of 2¾mm (US 2) knitting needles
- Double-pointed 2¾mm (US 2) knitting needles (for tail and for holding stitches)
- 20g (¾oz) of Rowan Pure Wool 4ply in Black 404 (bl)
- 5g (⅛oz) of Rowan Pure Wool 4ply in Snow 412 (sn)
- Tiny amount of Rowan Pure Wool 4ply in Gerbera 454 (ge) for eyes
- 3 pipecleaners for legs and tail
- Black thread for whiskers

Abbreviations
See page 172.
See page 172 for Wrap and Turn Method.

Right Back Leg
With sn, cast on 7 sts.
Beg with a k row, work 2 rows st st.
Row 3: Inc, k2tog, k1, k2tog, inc. (7 sts)
Row 4: Purl.
Cont in bl.
Row 5: Inc, k2tog, k1, k2tog, inc.* (7 sts)
Work 3 rows st st.
Row 9: K2, inc, k1, inc, k2. (9 sts)
Row 10: Purl.

Row 11: K3, inc, k1, inc, k3. (11 sts)
Row 12: P2tog, p2, inc, p1, inc, p2, p2tog. (11 sts)
Row 13: K2tog, inc, k1, inc, k1, inc, k1, inc, k2tog. (13 sts)
Row 14: Purl.
Row 15: K5, inc, k1, inc, k5. (15 sts)
Row 16: Purl.
Row 17: K6, inc, k1, inc, k6. (17 sts)
Row 18: Purl.
Row 19: K7, inc, k1, inc, k7. (19 sts)
Row 20: Purl.**
Row 21: Cast (bind) off 9 sts, k to end (hold 10 sts on spare needle for Right Side of Body).

Left Back Leg
Work as for Right Back Leg to **.
Row 21: K10, cast (bind) off 9 sts (hold 10 sts on spare needle for Left Side of Body).

Right Front Leg
Work as for Right Back Leg to *.
Work 5 rows st st.
Row 11: Inc, k5, inc. (9 sts)
Row 12: Purl.
Row 13: K3, inc, k1, inc, k3. (11 sts)
Row 14: Purl.
Row 15: K4, inc, k1, inc, k4. (13 sts)
Row 16: Purl.
Row 17: K5, inc, k1, inc, k5. (15 sts)
Row 18: Purl.***
Row 19: Cast (bind) off 7 sts, k to end (hold 8 sts on spare needle for Right Side of Body).

Left Front Leg
As Right Front Leg to ***.
Row 19: K8, cast (bind) off 7 sts (hold 8 sts on spare needle for Left Side of Body).

Right Side of Body
Row 1: With bl, cast on 1 st, with RS facing k8 from spare needle of Right Front Leg, cast on 7 sts. (16 sts)

Front Legs
When sewing tummy to body, make sure that the front legs are level at the chest.

Row 2: Purl.
Row 3: Inc, k15, cast on 8 sts. (25 sts)
Row 4: Purl.
Row 5: K25, with RS facing k10 from spare
needle of Right Back Leg, cast on 1 st.
(36 sts)
Row 6: Purl.
Row 7: Inc, k35. (37 sts)
Work 5 rows st st.
Row 13: K2tog, k35. (36 sts; place contrast
marker at neck end)
Row 14: Purl.
Row 15: K2tog, k34. (35 sts)
Row 16: Purl.
Row 17: K2tog, k33. (34 sts)
Row 18: P32, p2tog. (33 sts)
Row 19: K2tog, k29, k2tog. (31 sts)
Row 20: P2tog, p29. (30 sts)
Row 21: Cast (bind) off 10 sts, k18 icos,
k2tog. (19 sts)
Cast (bind) off.

Left Side of Body

Row 1: With bl, cast on 1 st, with WS facing
p8 from spare needle of Left Front Leg, cast
on 7 sts. (16 sts)
Row 2: Knit.
Row 3: Inc, p15, cast on 8 sts. (25 sts)
Row 4: Knit.
Row 5: P25, with WS facing p10 from
spare needle of Left Back Leg, cast on
1 st. (36 sts)
Row 6: Knit.
Row 7: Inc, p35. (37 sts)
Work 5 rows st st.
Row 13: P2tog, p35. (36 sts; place contrast
marker at neck end)
Row 14: Knit.
Row 15: P2tog, p34. (35 sts)
Row 16: Knit.
Row 17: P2tog, p33. (34 sts)
Row 18: K32, k2tog. (33 sts)
Row 19: P2tog, p29, p2tog. (31 sts)
Row 20: K2tog, k29. (30 sts)

Row 21: Cast (bind) off 10 sts, p18 icos,
p2tog. (19 sts)
Cast (bind) off.

Neck and Head

Row 1: With bl and RS facing, cast on 1 st,
pick up and k8 sts from row ends at neck
from marker of Right Side of Body, then pick
up and k8 sts from row ends of neck from
marker of Left Side of Body, inc into last of
these 8 sts. (18 sts)
Row 2: Purl.
Row 3: K5, inc, k6, inc, k5. (20 sts)
Row 4: Purl.
Row 5: K16, w&t (leave 4 sts on left-hand
needle unworked).

Body

For that sleek cat look, stroke
the cat's body to smooth
it out after stuffing.

Row 6: Working top of head on centre 12 sts only, p12, w&t.
Row 7: K12, w&t.
Rep last 2 rows once more.
Row 10: P12, w&t.
Row 11: K16. (20 sts on right-hand needle)
Row 12: Purl.
Row 13: K17, w&t (leave 3 sts on left-hand needle unworked).
Row 14: Working top of head on centre 14 sts only, p14, w&t.
Row 15: K14, w&t.
Rep last 2 rows once more.
Row 18: P14, w&t.
Row 19: K17. (20 sts in total)
Row 20: P2tog, p3, [p2tog, p2] twice, p2tog, p3, p2tog. (15 sts)
Row 21: K1, k2tog, k2, k2tog, k1, k2tog, k2, k2tog, k1. (11 sts)

Row 22: P2, p2tog, p3, p2tog, p2. (9 sts)
Row 23: Knit.
Row 24: P2, p2tog, p1, p2tog, p2. (7 sts)
Cast (bind) off.

Tummy
With bl, cast on 3 sts.
Beg with a k row, work 12 rows st st.
Row 13: Inc, k1, inc. (5 sts)
Work 31 rows st st.
Join in sn.
Row 45: K2bl, k1sn, k2bl.
Row 46: P1bl, p3sn, p1bl.
Cont in sn.
Work 20 rows st st.
Row 67: K2tog, k1, k2tog. (3 sts)
Work 3 rows st st.
Row 71: K3tog and fasten off.

Tail
With double-pointed needles and bl, cast on 6 sts.
Work in i-cord as folls:
Knit 20 rows.
Row 21: K2tog, k2, k2tog. (4 sts)
Knit 6 rows.
Row 28: [K2tog] twice. (2 sts)
Row 29: K2tog and fasten off.

Ear
(make 2 the same)
With bl, cast on 5 sts.
Beg with a k row, work 3 rows st st.
Row 4: K2tog, k1, k2tog. (3 sts)
Work 3 rows st st.
Row 8: K3tog and fasten off.

To Make Up
SEWING IN ENDS Sew in ends, leaving ends from cast on and cast (bound) off rows for sewing up.
LEGS With WS together and whip stitch, fold each leg in half and sew up legs on RS, starting at paws.

Whiskers
To secure the whiskers, add a spot of glue on either side of the cat's muzzle if you wish.

HEAD Fold cast (bound) off row of head in half and sew from nose to chin.

BODY Sew along back of cat and around bottom.

TUMMY Sew cast on row of tummy to base of cat's bottom (where legs begin), and sew cast (bound) off row to nose. Ease and sew tummy to fit body. Leave a 2.5cm (1in) gap between front and back legs on one side.

STUFFING Pipecleaners are used to stiffen the legs and help bend them into shape. Fold a pipecleaner into a U-shape and measure against front two legs. Cut to fit approximately, leaving an extra 2.5cm (1in) at both ends. Fold these ends over to stop the pipecleaner poking out of the paws. Roll a little stuffing around pipecleaner and slip into body, one end down each front leg. Repeat with second pipecleaner and back legs. Starting at the head, stuff the cat firmly, then sew up the gap. Mould body into shape.

TAIL Cut a pipecleaner to length of tail, plus a small amount in order to turn over the ends. Insert pipecleaner into tail, then attach cast on row of tail to start of bottom and bend tail into shape.

EARS With purl side facing forwards, sew cast on row of each ear to top of head, with 4 sts between ears.

EYES With ge, sew elongated 5-loop French knots, working each knot over 2 sts at a slight angle towards the nose. With bl, make a stitch over centre of French knots.

WHISKERS Cut six 5cm (2in) lengths of black thread. Thread these through cheeks, then trim.

Goose

There are many varieties of goose, but ours is the classic farmyard domestic variety. The most aggressive of poultry, geese were alleged to have saved Rome from the Gauls around 390BCE. Geese feature in many legends and fairytales, laying golden eggs, drawing chariots and changing into princesses. Their feathers also make a lovely filling for pillows and duvets.

Goose

You can make the goose more stable with the help of a cocktail stick pushed up the back of the leg and used like a high heel.

Measurements
Length: 10cm (4in)
Height to top of head: 16cm (6¼in)

Materials
- Pair of 2¾mm (US 2) knitting needles
- Double-pointed 2¾mm (US 2) knitting needles (for legs and for holding stitches)
- 5g (⅛oz) of Rowan Pure Wool 4ply in Jaipur 463 (ja)
- 25g (1oz) of Rowan Pure Wool 4ply in Snow 412 (sn)
- 2 pipecleaners for legs and feet
- 2 cocktail sticks or wooden kebab sticks to support legs
- 2 tiny black beads for eyes and sewing needle and black thread for sewing on

Abbreviations
See page 172.
See page 172 for I-cord Technique.

Leg and Foot
(make 2 the same)
With double-pointed needles and ja, cast on 4 sts.
Work i-cord as folls:
Knit 8 rows.
Shape feet
Row 9: Inc, k2, inc. (6 sts)

Row 10: Purl.
Row 11: Inc, k4, inc. (8 sts)
Row 12: Purl.
Row 13: Inc, k6, inc. (10 sts)
Row 14: Purl.
Knit 3 rows.
Row 18: P2tog, p6, p2tog. (8 sts)
Row 19: Knit.
Row 20: P2tog, p4, p2tog. (6 sts)
Row 21: Knit.
Row 22: P2tog, p2, p2tog. (4 sts)
Cast (bind) off.

Right Side of Body and Head
With sn, cast on 5 sts.
Row 1: Inc, k4. (6 sts)
Row 2: Purl.
Row 3: Inc, k4, inc. (8 sts)
Row 4: P8, cast on 4 sts. (12 sts)
Row 5: K11, inc. (13 sts)
Row 6: P13, cast on 2 sts. (15 sts)
Row 7: K14, inc. (16 sts)
Row 8: Purl.
Row 9: Inc, k14, inc. (18 sts)
Row 10: P18, cast on 2 sts. (20 sts)
Row 11: Knit.
Row 12: Purl.
Row 13: Inc, k18, inc. (22 sts)
Row 14: P22, cast on 2 sts. (24 sts)
Row 15: Knit.
Row 16: Purl.
Row 17: K23, inc. (25 sts)
Row 18: Purl.
Row 19: Knit.
Row 20: Inc, p24. (26 sts)
Row 21: K25, inc. (27 sts)
Row 22: Purl.
Row 23: Knit.
Row 24: Purl.
Row 25: Inc, k26. (28 sts)
Row 26: Purl.
Row 27: Cast (bind) off 5 sts, k to end. (23 sts)
Row 28: P21, p2tog. (22 sts)

Feet
Use pipecleaners to make a triangle for the webbed feet.

Row 29: Cast (bind) off 4 sts, k to end. (18 sts)
Row 30: P2tog, p16. (17 sts)
Row 31: Cast (bind) off 3 sts, k to end. (14 sts)
Row 32: Purl.
Row 33: Cast (bind) off 3 sts, k9 icos, k2tog. (10 sts)
Row 34: P2tog, p6, p2tog. (8 sts)
Row 35: K2tog, k6. (7 sts)
Row 36: Purl.
Work 6 rows st st.
Row 43: Inc, k4, k2tog. (7 sts)
Work 5 rows st st.
Row 49: Inc, k4, k2tog. (7 sts)
Row 50: Purl.
Row 51: K2tog, k5, cast on 3 sts. (9 sts)
Row 52: Purl.
Row 53: K2tog, k7. (8 sts)
Row 54: Purl.
Row 55: K2tog, k4, k2tog. (6 sts)
Row 56: P2tog, p2, p2tog. (4 sts)
Cast (bind) off 4 sts.

Left Side of Body and Head

With sn, cast on 5 sts.
Row 1: Inc, p4. (6 sts)
Row 2: Knit.
Row 3: Inc, p4, inc. (8 sts)
Row 4: K8, cast on 4 sts. (12 sts)
Row 5: P11, inc. (13 sts)
Row 6: K13, cast on 2 sts. (15 sts)
Row 7: P14, inc. (16 sts)
Row 8: Knit.
Row 9: Inc, p14, inc. (18 sts)
Row 10: K18, cast on 2 sts. (20 sts)
Row 11: Purl.
Row 12: Knit.
Row 13: Inc, p18, inc. (22 sts)
Row 14: K22, cast on 2 sts. (24 sts)
Row 15: Purl.
Row 16: Knit.
Row 17: P23, inc. (25 sts)
Row 18: Knit.

Row 19: Purl.
Row 20: Inc, k24. (26 sts)
Row 21: P25, inc. (27 sts)
Row 22: Knit.
Row 23: Purl.
Row 24: Knit.
Row 25: Inc, p26. (28 sts)
Row 26: Knit.
Row 27: Cast (bind) off 5 sts, p to end. (23 sts)
Row 28: K21, k2tog. (22 sts)
Row 29: Cast (bind) off 4 sts, p to end. (18 sts)
Row 30: K2tog, k16. (17 sts)

Wings

Attach the wings at an angle to the body and make sure they are symmetrical on each side.

Row 31: Cast (bind) off 3 sts, p to end. (14 sts)
Row 32: Knit.
Row 33: Cast (bind) off 3 sts, p9 icos, p2tog. (10 sts)
Row 34: K2tog, k6, k2tog. (8 sts)
Row 35: P2tog, p6. (7 sts)
Row 36: Knit.
Work 6 rows st st.
Row 43: Inc, p4, p2tog. (7 sts)
Work 5 rows st st.
Row 49: Inc, p4, p2tog. (7 sts)
Row 50: Knit.
Row 51: P2tog, p5, cast on 3 sts. (9 sts)

Eyes

The goose has tiny black beads for eyes.

Row 52: Knit.
Row 53: P2tog, p7. (8 sts)
Row 54: Knit.
Row 55: P2tog, p4, p2tog. (6 sts)
Row 56: K2tog, k2, k2tog. (4 sts)
Cast (bind) off 4 sts.

Beak

With WS together and whip stitch, sew sides of body together along centre back, up back of neck and across top of head.
Row 1: With ja and RS facing, pick up and k10 sts across end of head.
Row 2: P4, p2tog, p4. (9 sts)
Row 3: Knit.
Row 4: Purl.
Row 5: K2tog, k5, k2tog. (7 sts)
Row 6: Purl.
Row 7: K2tog, k3, k2tog. (5 sts)
Row 8: Purl.
Row 9: K2tog, k1, k2tog. (3 sts)
Row 10: Purl.
Cast (bind) off.

Wing

(make 2 the same)
With sn, cast on 6 sts.
Work 2 rows of k1, p1 rib.
Row 3: Inc, rib 4, inc. (8 sts)
Row 4: Rib.
Row 5: Inc, rib 6, inc. (10 sts)
Row 6: Rib.
Row 7: Inc, rib 8, inc. (12 sts)
Row 8: Rib.
Row 9: Inc, rib 10, inc. (14 sts)
Work 6 rows rib.
Row 16: Cast (bind) off 2 sts, rib to end. (12 sts)
Row 17: Rib.
Row 18: Cast (bind) off 2 sts, rib to end. (10 sts)
Row 19: Rib.
Row 20: Cast (bind) off 2 sts, rib to end. (8 sts)

Row 21: Rib.
Row 22: Cast (bind) off 2 sts, rib to end.
(6 sts)
Row 23: Rib.
Row 24: Cast (bind) off 2 sts, rib to end.
(4 sts)
Row 25: Rib.
Row 26: Cast (bind) off 2 sts, rib to end.
(2 sts)
Row 27: K2tog and fasten off.

To Make Up

SEWING IN ENDS Sew in ends, leaving ends from cast on and cast (bound) off rows for sewing up.
BODY With WS together and whip stitch, sew two halves of body together from tail, along bottom of body and up front including beak, leaving a 2.5cm (1in) gap.
STUFFING Stuff the goose firmly, then sew up the gap. Mould body into shape.
LEGS AND FEET Thread a pipecleaner through each i-cord leg and shape lower end into a triangle to form a webbed foot. Sew foot around the pipecleaner. Push other end of pipecleaner through base of body approx 1cm (¼in) apart. Sew legs to body. Insert wooden sticks up backs of legs and into body; these act as heels to help stabilize the goose.
WINGS Sew wings to body with long end at the top and approx 3 sts from back of neck and 3 rows down from centre back, with end of wing approx 6 rows down from centre back.
EYES Sew on black beads for eyes positioned as in photograph.

Gosling

Baby geese look nothing like their parents. They appear ungainly and badly designed, but at the same time fluffy and adorable. The collective noun for a group of geese on the ground is a gaggle, when in flight a skein and when flying close together a plump. Goslings don't feature much in literature and the best known is definitely Ryan.

Gosling

It's quite difficult to get the gosling to stand up as he's top heavy, so use the cocktail sticks to stabilize him.

Legs and Feet
Manipulate the legs and feet after finishing to help the gosling stand up.

Measurements

Length: 10cm (4in)
Height to top of head: 10cm (4in)

Materials

- Pair of 2¾mm (US 2) knitting needles
- Double-pointed 2¾mm (US 2) knitting needles (for legs and for holding stitches)
- 5g (⅛oz) of Rowan Pure Wool 4ply in Shale 402 (sh)
- 10g (¼oz) of Rowan Kidsilk Haze in Cream 634 (cr)
- 10g (¼oz) of Rowan Kidsilk Haze in Essence 663 (ec)

NOTE: some of this animal uses 1 strand of cr and 1 strand of ec held together, and this is called crec

- 2 pipecleaners for legs and feet
- 2 cocktail sticks or wooden kebab sticks to support legs
- 2 tiny black beads for eyes and sewing needle and black thread for sewing on

Abbreviations

See page 172.
See page 172 for I-cord Technique.

Leg and Foot

(make 2 the same)

With double-pointed needles and sh, cast on 4 sts.

Work i-cord as folls:

Knit 8 rows.

Shape feet

Row 9: Inc, k2, inc. (6 sts)

Row 10: Purl.

Row 11: Inc, k4, inc. (8 sts)

Row 12: Purl.

Knit 3 rows.

Row 16: P2tog, p4, p2tog. (6 sts)

Row 17: Knit.

Row 18: P2tog, p2, p2tog. (4 sts)

Row 19: Knit.

Cast (bind) off.

Right Side of Body and Head

With crec, cast on 5 sts.

Row 1: Inc, k4. (6 sts)

Row 2: Purl.

Row 3: Inc, k4, inc. (8 sts)

Row 4: P8, cast on 2 sts. (10 sts)

Row 5: K9, inc. (11 sts)

Row 6: Inc, p9, inc. (13 sts)

Row 7: Inc, k11, inc. (15 sts)

Row 8: Inc, p13, inc. (17 sts)

Row 9: K16, inc. (18 sts)

Row 10: P18, cast on 2 sts. (20 sts)

Row 11: Knit.

Row 12: Purl.

Row 13: Inc, k18, inc. (22 sts)

Row 14: P22, cast on 2 sts. (24 sts)

Row 15: Knit.

Row 16: Cast (bind) off 3 sts, p to end. (21 sts)

Row 17: K19, k2tog. (20 sts)

Row 18: Cast (bind) off 5 sts, p to end. (15 sts)

Row 19: Inc, k12, k2tog. (15 sts)

Row 20: Cast (bind) off 6 sts, p to end. (9 sts)

Row 21: K2tog, k7. (8 sts)

Row 22: P2tog, p6. (7 sts)

Row 23: K5, k2tog. (6 sts)

Row 24: Inc, p3, p2tog. (6 sts)

Row 25: Knit.

Row 26: P4, p2tog, cast on 4 sts. (9 sts)

Row 27: Knit.

Row 28: Purl.

Row 29: K7, k2tog. (8 sts)

Row 30: Inc, p7. (9 sts)

Row 31: K2tog, k3, inc, k3. (9 sts)

Row 32: Inc, p6, p2tog. (9 sts)

Row 33: K2tog, k5, k2tog. (7 sts)

Row 34: P2tog, p3, p2tog. (5 sts)

Cast (bind) off.

Left Side of Body and Head

With crec, cast on 5 sts.

Row 1: Inc, p4. (6 sts)

Row 2: Knit.

Row 3: Inc, p4, inc. (8 sts)

Row 4: K8, cast on 2 sts. (10 sts)

Row 5: P9, inc. (11 sts)

Row 6: Inc, k9, inc. (13 sts.)

Row 7: Inc, p11, inc. (15 sts)

Row 8: Inc, k13, inc. (17 sts)

Row 9: P16, inc. (18 sts)

Row 10: K18, cast on 2 sts. (20 sts)

Row 11: Purl.

Row 12: Knit.

Row 13: Inc, p18, inc. (22 sts)

Row 14: K22, cast on 2 sts. (24 sts)

Row 15: Purl.

Row 16: Cast (bind) off 3 sts, k to end. (21 sts)

Row 17: P19, p2tog. (20 sts)

Row 18: Cast (bind) off 5 sts, k to end. (15 sts)

Row 19: Inc, p12, p2tog. (15 sts)

Row 20: Cast (bind) off 6 sts, k to end. (9 sts)

Row 21: P2tog, p7. (8 sts)

Row 22: K2tog, k6. (7 sts)

Row 23: P5, p2tog. (6 sts)

Row 24: Inc, k3, k2tog. (6 sts)

Row 25: Purl.

Row 26: K4, k2tog, cast on 4 sts. (9 sts)

Eyes
The gosling has both French knots and black beads for eyes. The beads are optional.

Row 27: Purl.
Row 28: Knit.
Row 29: P7, p2tog. (8 sts)
Row 30: Inc, k7. (9 sts)
Row 31: P2tog, p3, inc, p3. (9 sts)
Row 32: Inc, k6, k2tog. (9 sts)
Row 33: P2tog, p5, p2tog. (7 sts)
Row 34: K2tog, k3, k2tog. (5 sts)
Cast (bind) off.

Beak
With WS together and whip stitch, sew sides of body together along centre back, up back

of neck and across top of head.
Row 1: With sh and RS facing, pick up and k6 sts across end of head.
Row 2: P2, p2tog, p2. (5 sts)
Row 3: K2tog, k1, k2tog. (3 sts)
Row 4: Purl.
Row 5: K2tog, k1. (2 sts)
Row 6: P2tog and fasten off.

Wing
(make 2 the same)
With crec, cast on 2 sts.
Beg with a k row, cont in st st.

Row 1: [Inc] twice. (4 sts)
Row 2: Purl.
Row 3: K1, [inc] twice, k1. (6 sts)
Row 4: Purl.
Row 5: K1, inc, k2, inc, k1. (8 sts)
Work 5 rows st st.
Cast (bind) off.

To Make Up

SEWING IN ENDS Sew in ends, leaving ends from cast on and cast (bound) off rows for sewing up.

BODY With WS together and whip stitch, sew two halves of body together from tail, along bottom of body and up front including beak, leaving a 2.5cm (1in) gap.

STUFFING Stuff the gosling firmly, then sew up the gap. Mould body into shape.

LEGS AND FEET Thread a pipecleaner through each i-cord leg and shape lower end into a triangle to form a webbed foot. Sew foot around the pipecleaner. Push other end of pipecleaner through base of body approx 1cm (¼in) apart. Sew legs to body. Insert wooden sticks up backs of legs and into body; these act as heels to help stabilize the gosling.

WINGS Sew wings to body with knit side uppermost and angled up towards back.

EYES With sh, sew 2-loop French knots positioned 3 sts back from beak and 2 rows down from top of head. Sew black beads on top of knots.

Goat

Goats are one of the oldest domestic animals. They are extremely curious, intelligent and fun-loving, and they can climb trees. Goats explore things with their upper lip and tongue, so beware as they will nibble and sometimes eat anything they're unacquainted with. Goats are very useful – we use their milk, hair and skin, and their meat is popular in West Indian cooking. The Rolling Stones made the legendary album *Goats Head Soup* in Jamaica in 1973.

Goat

Fragile and bony,
the goat is one of our
favourite animals.

Measurements
Length: 22cm (8¾in)
Height to top of horns: 16cm (6¼in)

Materials
- Pair of 3¼mm (US 3) knitting needles
- Double-pointed 3¼mm (US 3) knitting needles (for holding stitches)
- Pair of 2¾mm (US 2) knitting needles
- 5g (⅛oz) of Rowan Cocoon in Polar 801 (po)
- 30g (1¼oz) of Rowan Cocoon in Tundra 808 (tu)
- 5g (⅛oz) of Rowan Pure Wool 4ply in Shale 402 (sh)
- Tiny amount of Rowan Pure Wool 4ply in Black 404 (bl) for eyes
- 2 pipecleaners for legs and horns
- 2 tiny black beads for eyes and sewing needle and black thread for sewing on

Abbreviations
See page 172.
See page 173 for Scarf Fringe Method.
See page 172 for Wrap and Turn Method.

Right Back Leg
With 3¼mm (US 3) needles and po, cast on 4 sts.
Beg with a k row, work 8 rows st st.
Cont in tu.
Row 9: K1, [inc] twice, k1. (6 sts)
Row 10: Purl.

Row 11: K1, inc, k2, inc, k1. (8 sts)
Row 12: Purl.**
Row 13: K1, inc, k4, inc, k1. (10 sts)
Row 14: Purl.
Row 15: K1, inc, k6, inc, k1. (12 sts)
Row 16: Purl.*
Row 17: Cast (bind) off 6 sts, k to end (hold 6 sts on spare needle for Right Side of Body).

Left Back Leg
Work as for Right Back Leg to *.
Row 17: K6, cast (bind) off 6 sts (hold 6 sts on spare needle for Left Side of Body).

Right Front Leg
Work as for Right Back Leg to **.
Row 13: K1, inc, k4, inc, k1. (10 sts)
Work 3 rows st st.***
Row 17: Cast (bind) off 5 sts, k to end (hold 5 sts on spare needle for Right Side of Body).

Left Front Leg
Work as for Right Front Leg to ***.
Row 17: K5, cast (bind) off 5 sts (hold 5 sts on spare needle for Left Side of Body).

Right Side of Body
With 3¼mm (US 3) needles and tu, cast on 14 sts.
Row 1: Knit.
Row 2: Inc, p12, inc. (16 sts)
Row 3: Inc, k15, with RS facing k6 from spare needle of Right Back Leg. (23 sts)
Row 4: P23, with WS facing p5 from spare needle of Right Front Leg. (28 sts)
Row 5: Inc, k5, inc, k6, inc, k6, inc, k7. (32 sts)
Row 6: Purl.
Row 7: Inc, k29, k2tog. (32 sts)
Row 8: Purl.
Row 9: Inc, k31. (33 sts)
Row 10: Purl.
Row 11: Inc, k30, k2tog. (33 sts)
Work 3 rows st st.

Row 15: Inc, k8, k2tog, k6, k2tog, k6, k2tog, k6. (31 sts)
Row 16: Inc, p30. (32 sts)
Row 17: Knit.
Row 18: P2tog, p30. (31 sts)
Row 19: K29, k2tog. (30 sts)
Row 20: P2tog, p20, turn (hold 8 sts on spare needle for Neck and Head).
Row 21: Cast (bind) off 9 sts, k to end. Cast (bind) off 12 sts.

Left Side of Body

With 3¼mm (US 3) needles and tu, cast on 14 sts.
Row 1: Purl.
Row 2: Inc, k12, inc. (16 sts)
Row 3: Inc, p15, with WS facing p6 from spare needle of Left Back Leg. (23 sts)
Row 4: K23, with RS facing k5 from spare needle of Left Front Leg. (28 sts)
Row 5: Inc, p5, inc, p6, inc, p6, inc, p7. (32 sts)
Row 6: Knit.
Row 7: Inc, p29, p2tog. (32 sts)
Row 8: Knit.
Row 9: Inc, p31. (33 sts)
Row 10: Knit.
Row 11: Inc, p30, p2tog. (33 sts)
Work 3 rows st st.
Row 15: Inc, p8, p2tog, p6, p2tog, p6, p2tog, p6. (31 sts)
Row 16: Inc, k30. (32 sts)
Row 17: Purl.
Row 18: K2tog, k30. (31 sts)
Row 19: P29, p2tog. (30 sts)
Row 20: K2tog, k20, turn (hold 8 sts on spare needle for Neck and Head).
Row 21: Cast (bind) off 9 sts, p to end. Cast (bind) off.

Neck and Head

Row 1: With 3¼mm (US 3) needles and tu and with RS facing, k8 from spare needle of Right Side of Body, then k8 from spare needle of Left Side of Body. (16 sts)

Body
Don't overstuff the goat as he should have a slightly bony feel.

Legs

You can stuff the legs more firmly to give them shape.

Row 2: P7, p2tog, p7. (15 sts)
Row 3: K1, k2tog, k9, k2tog, k1. (13 sts)
Row 4: Purl.
Row 5: K1, k2tog, k7, k2tog, k1. (11 sts)
Row 6: Purl.
Row 7: Inc, k8, w&t (leave 2 sts on left-hand needle unworked).
Row 8: Working on top of head centre 7 sts only, p7, w&t.
Join in po.
Row 9: K2po, k3tu, k2po, w&t.
Row 10: P2po, p3tu, p2po, w&t.
Row 11: K2po, k3tu, k2po, k1tu, inctu. (13 sts in total)
Row 12: P3tu, p2po, p3tu, p2po, p3tu.
Row 13: K4tu, k1po, k3tu, k1po, k1tu, w&t (leave 3 sts on left-hand needle unworked).
Row 14: Working top of head on centre 7 sts only, p1tu, p1po, p3tu, p1po, p1tu, w&t.
Row 15: K1tu, k1po, k3tu, k1po, k1tu, w&t.
Row 16: P1tu, p1po, p3tu, p1po, p1tu, w&t.
Row 17: K1tu, k1po, k3tu, k1po, k4tu. (13 sts)
Row 18: P2togtu, p2tu, p1po, p3tu, p1po, p2tu, p2togtu. (11 sts)
Row 19: K2togtu, k1tu, k1po, k3tu, k1po, k1tu, k2togtu. (9 sts)
Row 20: P2togtu, p1tu, p1po, p1tu, p1po, p1tu, p2togtu, k3, k2tog. (7 sts)
Row 21: K2togtu, k1po, k1tu, k1po, k2togtu. (5 sts)
Cont in po.
Row 22: P2tog, p1, p2tog. (3 sts)
Row 23: Knit.
Cast (bind) off 3 sts.

Tummy

With 3¼mm (US 3) needles and tu, cast on 1 st.
Beg with a k row, cont in st st.
Row 1: Inc. (2 sts)
Row 2: Purl.
Row 3: [Inc] twice. (4 sts)
Row 4: Purl.

Row 5: Inc, k2, inc. (6 sts)
Row 6: Purl.
Work 34 rows st st.
Row 41: K2tog, k2, k2tog. (4 sts)
Work 29 rows st st.
Row 71: [K2tog] twice. (2 sts)
Work 5 rows st st.
Join in po.
Work 4 rows st st.
Row 81: K2tog and fasten off.

Tail

With 3¼mm (US 3) needles and tu, cast on 4 sts.
Work 8 rows st st.
Row 9: [K2tog] twice.
Cast (bind) off.

Ear

(make 2 the same)
With 3¼mm (US 3) needles and tu, cast on 3 sts.
Beg with a k row, work 2 rows st st.
Row 3: K1, inc, k1. (4 sts)
Work 3 rows st st.
Row 7: [K2tog] twice. (2 sts)
Row 8: P2tog and fasten off.

Horn

(make 2 the same)
With 2¾mm (US 2) needles and sh, cast on 4 sts.
Beg with a k row, work 10 rows st st.
Row 11: K1, k2tog, k1. (3 sts)
Work 5 rows st st.
Cast (bind) off.

To Make Up

SEWING IN ENDS Sew in ends, leaving ends from cast on and cast (bound) off rows for sewing up.
LEGS With WS together and whip stitch, fold each leg in half and sew up legs on RS, starting at hooves.

BODY Sew along back of goat and 4cm (1½in) down bottom.

TUMMY Sew cast on row of tummy to where you have finished sewing down bottom, and sew cast (bound) off row to nose. Ease and sew tummy to fit body. Leave a 2.5cm (1in) gap between front and back legs on one side.

STUFFING Pipecleaners are used to stiffen the legs and help bend them into shape. Fold a pipecleaner into a U-shape and measure against front two legs. Cut to fit approximately, leaving an extra 2.5cm (1in) at both ends. Fold these ends over to stop the pipecleaner poking out of the hooves. Roll a little stuffing around pipecleaner and slip into body, one end down each front leg. Repeat with second pipecleaner and back legs. Starting at the head, stuff the goat, but do not overstuff as it looks more goat-like if slightly loosely stuffed, then sew up the gap. Mould body into shape.

TAIL Attach cast (bound) off row of tail to start of bottom.

EARS With purl side facing forwards, sew cast on row of each ear to where stripe in po yarn starts at top of head, with 3 sts between ears.

EYES With bl, sew 2-loop French knots positioned as in photograph, approx 5 rows down from ears on stripe in po. Sew black beads on top of knots.

HORNS Cut a 10cm (4in) length of leftover pipecleaner and push through top of head between ears. Wrap horns around protruding ends of pipecleaner and sew up. Sew horns to head, then bend into shape.

BEARD Cut two 4cm (1½in) lengths of po yarn and use crochet hook and Scarf Fringe Method (see page 173) to attach to end of chin, then fray yarn.

Hen

The hen, a female chicken, is a very useful and much-loved bird, producing eggs and used for meat. Very fashionable these days, exotic breeds of hens are kept for both their eggs and as pets. Hens live in flocks with certain birds dominating, so a 'pecking order' has to be established. Famous cartoon hens include Camilla, Gonzo the Great's girlfriend in *The Muppet Show*. Hens are equally popular characters in children's books, such as *The Little Red Hen* and the fable *Henny Penny*.

Hen

Easy to knit, the hen is one of the simplest animals to make.

Measurements

Length: 12cm (4¾in)
Height to top of head: 13cm (5in)

Materials

- Pair of 2¾mm (US 2) knitting needles
- 15g (½oz) of Rowan Fine Tweed in Dent 373 (dt)
- Small amount of Rowan Pure Wool 4ply in Kiss 436 (ks) for wattle and comb
- Small amount of Rowan Pure Wool 4ply in Gerbera 454 (ga) for beak, legs and claws
- 2 pipecleaners for legs and feet
- 2 tiny black beads for eyes and sewing needle and black thread for sewing on

Abbreviations

See page 172.
See page 173 for Loopy Stitch. Work 2-finger loopy stitch throughout pattern.
See page 172 for Wrap and Turn Method.
See page 173 for Leg and Claw Method.

Right Side of Body

With dt, cast on 10 sts.
Beg with a k row, work 2 rows st st.
Row 3: Inc, k8, inc. (12 sts)
Row 4: Inc, p10, inc. (14 sts)
Row 5: Inc, k12, inc. (16 sts)
Row 6: Purl.
Row 7: Inc, k15. (17 sts)
Row 8: Purl.

Row 9: Inc, k15, inc. (19 sts)
Row 10: Inc, p18, cast on 2 sts. (22 sts)
Row 11: Inc, k21. (23 sts)
Row 12: Purl.
Row 13: Inc, k22. (24 sts)
Row 14: Purl.
Row 15: Inc, k23. (25 sts)
Row 16: P24, inc. (26 sts)
Work 4 rows st st.
Row 21: K25, inc. (27 sts)
Work 3 rows st st.
Row 25: K2tog, k24, inc. (27 sts)
Row 26: Purl.
Row 27: K2tog, k24, inc. (27 sts)
Row 28: Purl.
Row 29: K10, cast (bind) off 4 sts, k11 icos, loopy st 1, k1 (hold 10 sts on spare needle for Neck and Head).
Row 30: Working on 13 sts for tail, purl.
Row 31: Cast (bind) off 3 sts, k6 icos, loopy st 1, k1, loopy st 1, inc. (11 sts)
Row 32: Purl.
Row 33: Cast (bind) off 3 sts, k2 icos, [loopy st 1, k1] 3 times. (8 sts)
Row 34: P6, p2tog. (7 sts)
Row 35: K2tog, loopy st 1, k1, loopy st 1, k2. (6 sts)
Row 36: Purl.
Row 37: K2tog, [loopy st 1, k1] twice. (5 sts)
Cast (bind) off.

Left Side of Body

With dt, cast on 10 sts.
Beg with p row, work 2 rows st st.
Row 3: Inc, p8, inc. (12 sts)
Row 4: Inc, k10, inc. (14 sts)
Row 5: Inc, p12, inc. (16 sts)
Row 6: Knit.
Row 7: Inc, p15. (17 sts)
Row 8: Knit.
Row 9: Inc, p15, inc. (19 sts)
Row 10: Inc, k18, cast on 2 sts. (22 sts)
Row 11: Inc, p21. (23 sts)
Row 12: Knit.

Head

Attach the wattles so that they hang
below the beak, and the comb so
that it sticks up on top of the head.

Row 13: Inc, p22. (24 sts)
Row 14: Knit.
Row 15: Inc, p23. (25 sts)
Row 16: K24, inc. (26 sts)
Work 4 rows st st.
Row 21: P25, inc. (27 sts)
Work 3 rows st st.
Row 25: P2tog, p24, inc. (27 sts)
Row 26: Knit.
Row 27: P2tog, p24, inc. (27 sts)
Row 28: Knit.
Row 29: P10, cast (bind) off 4 sts, p to end
(hold 10 sts on spare needle for Neck and
Head).
Row 30: Working on 13 sts for tail, k1,
loopy st 1, k11.
Row 31: Cast (bind) off 3 sts, p9, inc. (11 sts)
Row 32: K1, [loopy st 1, k1] twice, k6.
Row 33: Cast (bind) off 3 sts, p to end. (8 sts)
Row 34: [K1, loopy st 1] 3 times, k2tog.
(7 sts)
Row 35: P2tog, p5. (6 sts)
Row 36: [K1, loopy st 1] twice, k2.
Row 37: P2tog, p4. (5 sts)
Row 38: K2tog, loopy st 1 and cast (bind) off
last 2 sts worked, cast (bind) off rem sts.

Neck and Head

Row 1: With dt and RS facing, k10 from
spare needle of Right Side of Body, then
k10 from spare needle of Left Side of Body.
(20 sts)
Row 2: Purl.
Row 3: K2tog, k6, [k2tog] twice, k6, k2tog.
(16 sts)
Row 4: Purl.
Row 5: Knit.
Row 6: P6, [p2tog] twice, p6. (14 sts)
Row 7: K2tog, k10, k2tog. (12 sts)
Row 8: Purl.
Join in ks.
Row 9: K2togks, k1ks, k6dt, k1ks, k2togks.
(10 sts)
Row 10: P3ks, p4dt, p3ks.

Tail
To make the tail more luxurious, the loopy stitches can be knitted in different sizes.

Row 11: K3ks, k4dt, w&t (leave 3 sts on left-hand needle unworked).
Row 12: Working top of head on centre 4 sts only, p4dt, w&t.
Row 13: K4dt, w&t.
Row 14: P4dt, w&t.
Row 15: K4dt, k3ks. (10 sts in total)
Row 16: P2togks, p1ks, [p2togdt] twice, p1ks, p2togks. (6 sts)
Cont in ks.
Row 17: K2, k2tog, k2. (5 sts)
Row 18: P2tog, p1, p2tog. (3 sts)
Cast (bind) off.

Beak
With ga, cast on 5 sts.
Beg with a k row, work 2 rows st st.
Row 3: K2tog, k1, k2tog. (3 sts)
Row 4: Purl.
Row 5: K3tog and fasten off.

Wattle
(make 2 the same)
With ks, cast on 2 sts.
Knit 2 rows.
Row 3: [Inc] twice. (4 sts)
Knit 4 rows.
Row 8: [K2tog] twice. (2 sts)
Cast (bind) off.

Comb

With ks, cast on 6 sts.

Knit 1 row.

Picot edge cast (bind) off row: *Cast on 2 sts, cast (bind) off 4 sts, move last st from right-hand needle to left-hand needle.* Rep from * to * once more. (2 sts) Cast on 2 sts, cast (bind) off rem sts.

Leg and One Front Claw

(make 2 the same)

With ga, cast on 4 sts.

Beg with a k row, work 16 rows st st.

Cast (bind) off.

Front and Back Claws

(make 2 the same)

With ga, cast on 4 sts.

Beg with a k row, work 12 rows st st.

Cast (bind) off.

To Make Up

SEWING IN ENDS Sew in ends, leaving ends from cast on and cast (bound) off rows for sewing up.

BODY With WS together and whip stitch, sew two halves of body together, leaving a 2.5cm (1in) gap.

STUFFING Stuff the hen firmly, then sew up the gap. Mould body into shape.

LEGS AND FEET Using a 20cm (8in) length of pipecleaner and the Leg and Claw Method (see page 173), make up legs and feet. The hen's legs are 2cm (¾in) high. To attach the legs, push protruding ends of pipecleaners into base of body approx 4 rows apart.

BEAK With WS together, sew up beak and attach to head positioned as in photograph.

WATTLES Attach cast (bound) off row of wattles just below and to either side of beak.

COMB Sew cast on row along top of head.

EYES Sew on black beads positioned as in photograph.

Chick

Which came first, the chick or the egg? Chicks, fluffy and charming, take 21 days to hatch from their eggs. They symbolize new life and are often associated with Easter.

Chick

This little chick is cute
and really easy to knit.

Measurements

Length: 6cm (2½in)
Height to top of head: 7cm (2¾in)

Materials

- Pair of 2¾mm (US 2) knitting needles
- 10g (¼oz) of Rowan Kidsilk Haze
  in Essence 663 (ec) used DOUBLE
  throughout
- 5g (⅛oz) of Rowan Pure Wool 4ply in
  Jaipur 463 (ja) for legs and beak
- 2 pipecleaners for legs and feet
- 2 tiny black beads for eyes and sewing
  needle and black thread for sewing on

Abbreviations

See page 172.
See page 173 for Leg and Claw Method.

NOTE: work as directed, but to create a
chick as in photograph, make up body with
purl side as right side.

Body

Starting at the tail, with ec cast on 18 sts.
Row 1: Knit.
Row 2: P1, inc, p4, inc, p4, inc, p4, inc, p1.
(22 sts)
Row 3: Knit.
Row 4: P6, inc, p8, inc, p6. (24 sts)
Row 5: Knit.
Row 6: P1, inc, p6, inc, p6, inc, p6, inc, p1.
(28 sts)
Row 7: Knit.

Row 8: P10, inc, p6, inc, p10. (30 sts)
Row 9: Knit.
Row 10: P1, inc, p9, inc, p6, inc, p9, inc, p1.
(34 sts)
Row 11: Knit.
Row 12: P1, inc, p10, inc, p8, inc, p10, inc,
p1. (38 sts)
Row 13: Knit.
Row 14: P1, inc, p13, p2tog, p4, p2tog, p13,
inc, p1. (38 sts)
Row 15: Knit.
Row 16: P1, inc, p6, p2tog, p5, p2tog, p4,
p2tog, p5, p2tog, p6, inc, p1. (36 sts)
Row 17: K8, k2tog, k4, k2tog, k4, k2tog, k4,
k2tog, k8. (32 sts)
Row 18: P6, p2tog, p4, p2tog, p4, p2tog, p4,
p2tog, p6. (28 sts)
Row 19: K2tog, k5, k2tog, k4, k2tog, k4,
k2tog, k5, k2tog. (24 sts)
Row 20: P8, p2tog, p4, p2tog, p8. (22 sts)
Row 21: K2tog, k18, k2tog. (20 sts)
Row 22: Purl.
Row 23: K2tog, k16, k2tog. (18 sts)

Eyes

This little chick has beads for eyes,
but you can make French knots
with black yarn if you prefer.

Work 3 rows st st.
Row 27: P2, p2tog, p2, p2tog, p2, p2tog, p2,
p2tog, p2. (14 sts)
Row 28: Purl.
Row 29: K2tog, k1, [k2tog] 4 times, k1,
k2tog. (8 sts)
Row 30: [P2tog] 4 times. (4 sts)
Row 31: K4tog and fasten off.

Beak

With ja, cast on 4 sts.
Beg with a k row, work 2 rows st st.
Row 3: [K2tog] twice. (2 sts)
Row 4: P2tog and fasten off.

Leg and One Front Claw

(make 2 the same)
With ja, cast on 4 sts.
Beg with a k row, work 12 rows st st.
Cast (bind) off.

Front and Back Claws

(make 2 the same)
With ja, cast on 4 sts.
Beg with a k row, work 10 rows st st.
Cast (bind) off.

To Make Up

SEWING IN ENDS Sew in ends, leaving ends
from cast on and cast (bound) off rows for
sewing up.
BODY With knit sides together and whip
stitch, fold body in half and sew together,
leaving a 2.5cm (1in) gap.
STUFFING Stuff the chick firmly, then sew
up the gap. Mould body into shape.
LEGS AND FEET Using an 18cm (7in)
length of pipecleaner and the Leg and
Claw Method (see page 173), make up legs
and feet. The chick's legs are 1cm (¼in)
high. To attach the legs, push protruding
ends of pipecleaners into base of body
approx 4 rows apart.
BEAK With knit sides together, sew up
beak and attach to head as in photograph.
EYES Sew on black beads positioned as
in photograph.

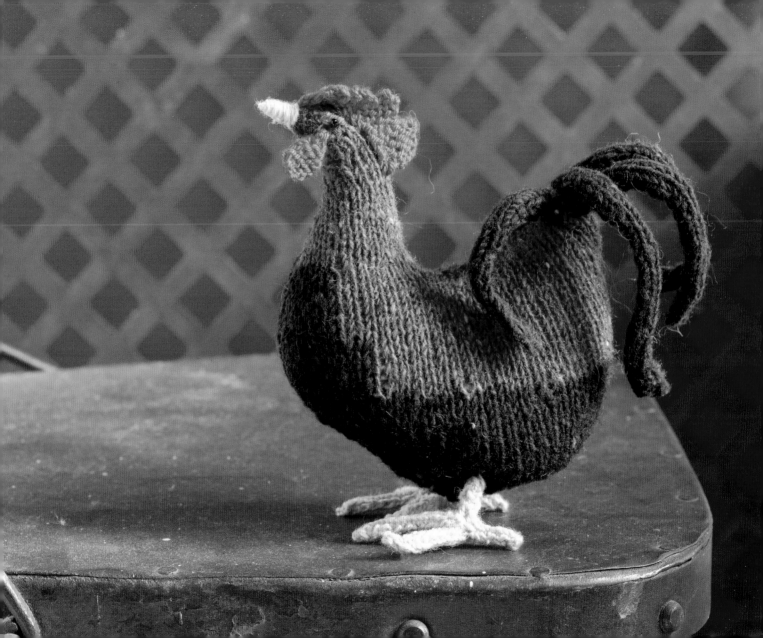

Cockerel

The cockerel, also known as a rooster, is the alarm clock of poultry. He is a magnificent bird, pugnacious and territorial, and protects his many wives ferociously. Cockfighting used to be a popular 'sport' in England but has fortunately been stamped out. The cockerel, which signifies vigilance, is the symbol for Chianti Classico, Tottenham Hotspur and France. Famous cartoon cockerels include Rocky, the flying rooster in *Chicken Run*, and Foghorn J. Leghorn from the *Looney Tunes*.

Cockerel

Splendid and elaborate,
the cockerel is relatively
easy to knit.

Measurements
Length: 17cm (6¾in)
Height to top of head: 17cm (6¾in)

Materials
- Pair of 2¾mm (US 2) knitting needles
- Double-pointed 2¾mm (US 2) knitting
  needles (for holding stitches)
- 20g (¾oz) of Rowan Fine Tweed in
  Dent 373 (dt)
- 20g (¾oz) of Rowan Fine Tweed in
  Askrigg 365 (as)
- 5g (⅛oz) of Rowan Pure Wool 4ply in
  Kiss 436 (ks)
- 5g (⅛oz) of Rowan Pure Wool 4ply in
  Gerbera 454 (ga)
- 2 pipecleaners for legs, feet and tail
  feathers
- 2 tiny black beads for eyes and sewing
  needle and black thread for sewing on
- Glue stick for beak

Abbreviations
See page 172.

Right Side of Body and Head
With as, cast on 13 sts.
Beg with a k row, work 2 rows st st.
Row 3: Inc, k11, inc. (15 sts)
Row 4: Inc, p13, inc. (17 sts)
Row 5: Inc, k15, inc. (19 sts)
Row 6: Purl.

Row 7: Inc, k18. (20 sts)
Row 8: Purl.
Row 9: Inc, k18, inc. (22 sts)
Row 10: Inc, p21, cast on 2 sts. (25 sts)
Row 11: Inc, k24. (26 sts)
Row 12: Purl.
Row 13: Inc, k25. (27 sts)
Row 14: P26, inc. (28 sts)
Join in dt.
Row 15: Incas, k18as, k9dt. (29 sts)
Row 16: P12dt, p16as, incas. (30 sts)
Row 17: K15as, k15dt.
Row 18: P18dt, p12as.
Row 19: K9as, k21dt.
Row 20: P21dt, p9as.
Row 21: Rep row 19.
Row 22: Rep row 20.
Row 23: K9as, k20dt, incdt. (31 sts)
Row 24: P22dt, p9as.
Row 25: K7as, k24dt.
Row 26: P24dt, p7as.
Row 27: K7as, k24dt.
Row 28: P24dt, p7as.
Row 29: K2togas, k5as, k23dt, incdt. (31 sts)
Row 30: P25dt, p6as.
Row 31: K2togas, k4as, k24dt, incdt. (31 sts)
Row 32: P26dt, p5as.
Row 33: K5as, k8dt (hold 13 sts on spare
needle for Neck and Head), cast (bind) off
4 sts dt, k14dt icos. (14 sts)
Cont in dt.
Row 34: Purl.
Row 35: Cast (bind) off 4 sts, k9 icos, inc.
(11 sts)
Row 36: Purl.
Row 37: Cast (bind) off 3 sts, k to end. (8 sts)
Row 38: P6, p2tog. (7 sts)
Row 39: K2tog, k5. (6 sts)
Row 40: Purl.
Shape tail feathers
Join in as.
Row 41: K2togdt, incas, turn and work on
these 2 sts only with as.
Row 42: [Inc] twice. (4 sts)

Row 43: Inc, k2, inc. (6 sts)
Working on these 6 sts, work 11 rows st st.
Row 55: K2tog, k2, k2tog. (4 sts)
Work 27 rows st st.
Row 83: [K2tog] twice. (2 sts)
Row 84: P2tog and fasten off.
Row 85: Rejoin dt to rem sts (row 41), incas,
turn and work on these 2 sts only with as.
Rep rows 42–84 once more.
Row 129: Rejoin dt to rem sts (row 41), k2.
Row 130: P2tog and fasten off.

Left Side of Body and Head
With as, cast on 13 sts.
Beg with a p row, work 2 rows st st.
Row 3: Inc, p11, inc. (15 sts)
Row 4: Inc, k13, inc. (17 sts)
Row 5: Inc, p15, inc. (19 sts)
Row 6: Knit.
Row 7: Inc, p18. (20 sts)
Row 8: Knit.
Row 9: Inc, p18, inc. (22 sts)
Row 10: Inc, k21, cast on 2 sts. (25 sts)
Row 11: Inc, p24. (26 sts)
Row 12: Knit.
Row 13: Inc, p25. (27 sts)
Row 14: K26, inc. (28 sts)
Join in dt.
Row 15: Incas, p18as, p9dt. (29 sts)
Row 16: K12dt, k16as, incas. (30 sts)
Row 17: P15as, p15dt.
Row 18: K18dt, k12as.
Row 19: P9as, p21dt.
Row 20: K21dt, k9as.
Row 21: Rep row 19.
Row 22: Rep row 20.
Row 23: P9as, p20dt, incdt. (31 sts)
Row 24: K22dt, k9as.
Row 25: P7as, p24dt.
Row 26: K24dt, k7as.
Row 27: P7as, p24dt.
Row 28: K24dt, k7as.
Row 29: P2togas, p5as, p23dt, incdt. (31 sts)
Row 30: K25dt, k6as.

Head

The cockerel's comb will stand up on its own and the wattles will dangle downwards.

Row 31: P2togas, p4as, p24dt, incdt. (31 sts)
Row 32: K26dt, k5as.
Row 33: P5as, p8dt (hold 13 sts on spare needle for Neck and Head), cast (bind) off 4 sts dt, p14dt icos. (14 sts)
Cont in dt.
Row 34: Knit.
Row 35: Cast (bind) off 4 sts, p9 icos, inc. (11 sts)
Row 36: Knit.
Row 37: Cast (bind) off 3 sts, p to end. (8 sts)
Row 38: K6, k2tog. (7 sts)
Row 39: P2tog, p5. (6 sts)
Shape tail feathers
Join in as.
Row 40: K2togdt, incas, turn and work on these 2 sts only with as.

Row 41: [Inc] twice. (4 sts)
Row 42: Inc, k2, inc. (6 sts)
Working on these 6 sts sts work 11 rows st st.
Row 56: K2tog, k2, k2tog. (4 sts)
Work 27 rows st st.
Row 82: [K2tog] twice. (2 sts)
Row 83: P2tog and fasten off.
Row 84: Rejoin dt to rem sts (row 40), incas, turn and work on these 2 sts only with as. Rep rows 41–83 once more.
Row 128: Rejoin dt to rem sts (row 40), k2.
Row 129: P2tog and fasten off.

Neck and Head

Row 1: With dt, k13 from spare needle of Right Side of Body, then k13 from spare

Tail

The cockerel's tail feathers will need pressing. A pipecleaner inserted part of the way up each feather will help them to stand up.

needle of Left Side of Body. (26 sts)
Row 2: Purl.
Row 3: K2tog, k6, k2tog, k6, k2tog, k6, k2tog. (22 sts)
Row 4: Purl.
Row 5: Knit.
Row 6: Purl.
Row 7: K2tog, k8, k2tog, k8, k2tog. (19 sts)
Row 8: Purl.
Row 9: Knit.
Row 10: Purl.
Row 11: K2tog, k4, k2tog, k3, k2tog, k4, k2tog. (15 sts)
Row 12: Purl.
Work 2 rows st st.
Join in ks.
Row 15: K2togks, k1ks, k9dt, k1ks, k2togks. (13 sts)
Row 16: P4ks, p5dt, p4ks.
Row 17: K3ks, k7dt, w&t (leave 3 sts on left-hand needle unworked).
Row 18: Working top of head on these 7 sts only, p7dt, w&t.
Row 19: K7dt, w&t.
Row 20: P7dt, w&t.
Row 21: K7dt, k3ks. (13 sts in total)
Row 22: P2togks, p1ks, p2togdt, p3dt, p2togdt, p1ks, p2togks. (9 sts)
Row 23: K2ks, k5dt, w&t (leave 2 sts on left-hand needle unworked).
Row 24: Working top of head on these 5 sts only, p5dt, w&t.
Row 25: K5dt, w&t.
Row 26: P5dt, w&t.
Row 27: K5dt, k2ks. (9 sts in total)
Cont in dt.
Row 28: P2tog, p5, p2tog. (7 sts)
Row 29: K2tog, k3, k2tog. (5 sts)
Cast (bind) off.

Wattle

(make 2 the same)
With ks, cast on 5 sts.
Knit 3 rows.

Row 4: K2tog, k3. (4 sts)
Row 5: Knit.
Row 6: K2tog, k2. (3 sts)
Row 7: Knit.
Cast (bind) off.

Comb

With ks, cast on 5 sts.
Knit 2 rows.
Row 3: K4, inc. (6 sts)
Knit 2 rows.
Row 6: K5, inc. (7 sts)
Row 7: Cast (bind) off 3 sts, k to end. (4 sts)
Row 8: K4, cast on 2 sts. (6 sts)
Knit 2 rows.
Row 11: Cast (bind) off 2 sts, k to end. (4 sts)
Row 12: K3, inc. (6 sts)
Knit 2 rows.
Row 15: K3, k2tog. (4 sts)
Row 16: K2tog, k2. (3 sts)
Row 17: K3, cast on 2 sts. (5 sts)
Row 18: Knit.
Row 19: K3, k2tog. (4 sts)
Row 20: K2tog, k2. (3 sts)
Row 21: K1, k2tog. (2 sts)
Row 22: K2tog and fasten off.

Leg and Spur

(make 2 the same)
With ga, cast on 4 sts.
Beg with a k row, work 18 rows st st.
Cast (bind) off.

Outer Claws

(make 2 the same)
With ga, cast on 1 st.
Beg with a k row, cont in st st.
Row 1: Inc. (2 sts)
Row 2: Purl.
Row 3: [Inc] twice. (4 sts)
Work 23 rows st st.
Row 27: [K2tog] twice. (2 sts)
Row 28: Purl.
Row 29: K2tog and fasten off.

Middle Claw

(make 2 the same)
Work as for First Front Claw, but working
11 rows st st.
Cast (bind) off.

To Make Up

SEWING IN ENDS Sew in ends, leaving ends
from cast on and cast (bound) off rows for
sewing up.

BODY With WS together and whip stitch,
sew two halves of body together, leaving a
2.5cm (1in) gap.

STUFFING Stuff the cockerel firmly, then
sew up the gap. Mould body into shape.

LEGS AND FEET Using a 20cm (8in)
length of pipecleaner and the Leg and Claw
Method (see page 173), make up legs and
feet. The cockerel's legs are 2cm (¾in) high.
To attach the legs, push protruding ends
of pipecleaners into base of body approx
8 rows apart.

TAIL Press tail feathers and sew up 5cm
(2in) of each feather from bottom end. Insert
a short length of pipecleaner into each sewn
up section through bottom end; push other
end of pipecleaner into cockerel's bottom.
This makes the tail feathers stand up.

WATTLES Attach cast (bound) off row of
wattles to side of head, approx 2 rows down
from top of head and 4 sts from beak.

COMB Sew along top of head, starting at
beak end of head.

EYES Sew on black beads positioned as
in photograph.

BEAK Cut approx 2cm (¾in) length of
pipecleaner, bend in half and push into
beak end of cockerel's head. Smear with
glue and wrap ga yarn around it, then tie
and sew in ends.

Highland Cow

Originating from the Highlands of Scotland, this truly spectacular and hardy animal has a long coat to keep the heat in and the cold out. Expert foragers, Highland cows will eat plants that many other cattle won't. Hamish, 'an icon of the Scottish Highlands', was saved from the slaughterhouse during the BSE scare in the 1990s; campaigners argued that he was popular with children, who saw him as a pet. In 2010, Hamish hit the headlines again, when, on meeting his new companion Heather, he danced a 'Highland fling'. They now happily share a field.

Highland Cow

The Highland cow is a
difficult animal to knit,
but hugely rewarding.

Measurements
Length: 30cm (12in)
Height to top of head: 18cm (7in)

Materials
- Pair of 3¼mm (US 3) knitting needles
- Double-pointed 3¼mm (US 3) knitting
  needles (for tail and for holding stitches)
- Small amount of Rowan Creative Focus
  Worsted in Charcoal Heather 00402 (ch)
  for hooves, eyes and nose
- 35g (1⅜oz) of Rowan Creative Focus
  Worsted in Golden Heather 00018 (gh)
- 25g (1oz) of Rowan Kidsilk Haze in
  Fudge 658 (fu) used DOUBLE throughout
- 5g (⅛oz) Rowan Pure Wool DK in
  Clay 048 (cl)
- 3 pipecleaners for legs and horns

Abbreviations
See page 172.
See page 173 for Loopy Stitch. Work 3-finger
loopy stitch throughout pattern.
See page 172 for I-cord Technique.

Right Back Leg
With ch, cast on 11 sts.
Beg with a k row, work 2 rows st st.
Row 3: Inc, k2, k2tog, k1, k2tog, k2, inc.
(11 sts)
Cont in gh.
Row 4: Purl.

Row 5: K3, k2tog, k1, k2tog, k3.** (9 sts)
Work 8 rows st st.
Cont in fu.
Row 14: Purl.*
Row 15: K3, [loopy st 1, k1] 3 times.
Cont in gh.
Row 16: Purl.
Row 17: K3, inc, k1, inc, k3. (11 sts)
Row 18: Purl.
Row 19: Knit.
Cont in fu.
Row 20: Purl.
Row 21: K4, inc, loopy st 1, inc, [loopy st 1,
k1] twice. (13 sts)
Cont in gh.
Work 3 rows st st.
Row 25: K5, inc, k1, inc, k5. (15 sts)
Cont in fu.
Row 26: Purl.
Row 27: K6, [loopy st 1, k1] 4 times, k1.
Cont in gh.
Row 28: Purl.
Row 29: Cast (bind) off 7 sts, k to end (hold
8 sts on spare needle for Right Side of Body).

Left Back Leg
Work as for Right Back Leg to *.
Row 15: [K1, loopy st 1] 3 times, k3.
Cont in gh.
Row 16: Purl.
Row 17: K3, inc, k1, inc, k3. (11 sts)
Row 18: Purl.
Row 19: Knit.
Cont in fu.
Row 20: Purl.
Row 21: [K1, loopy st 1] twice, inc, loopy st 1,
inc, k4. (13 sts)
Cont in gh.
Work 3 rows st st.
Row 25: K5, inc, k1, inc, k5. (15 sts)
Cont in fu.
Row 26: Purl.
Row 27: [K1, loopy st 1] 4 times, k7.
Cont in gh.

Legs
If you make a small mistake, don't
reknit – it won't be noticeable
under all the loopy stitches.

Row 28: Purl.
Row 29: K8, cast (bind) off 7 sts (hold 8 sts on spare needle for Left Side of Body).

Right Front Leg

Work as for Right Back Leg to **.
Work 6 rows st st.
Cont in fu.
Row 12: Purl.
Row 13: K1, [loopy st 1, k1] 4 times.
Cont in gh.
Row 14: Purl.
Row 15: K3, inc, k1, inc, k3. (11 sts)
Row 16: Purl.
Row 17: Knit.
Cont in fu.
Row 18: Purl.
Row 19: [K1, loopy st 1] twice, inc, loopy st 1, inc, [loopy st 1, k1] twice. (13 sts)
Cont in gh.
Work 3 rows st st.***
Row 23: Cast (bind) off 6 sts, k to end (hold 7 sts on spare needle for Right Side of Body).

Left Front Leg

Work as for Right Front Leg to ***.
Row 23: K7, cast (bind) off 6 sts (hold 7 sts on spare needle for Left Side of Body).

Right Side of Body and Head

With gh, cast on 2 sts.
Row 1: Purl.
Row 2: [Inc] twice. (4 sts)
Row 3: Purl.
Row 4: Inc, k2, inc. (6 sts)
Row 5: Purl.
Row 6: Inc, k5, with RS facing k7 from spare needle of Right Front Leg, cast on 8 sts. (22 sts)
Row 7: Purl.
Cont in fu.
Row 8: Inc, [loopy st 1, k1] 10 times, k1, cast on 5 sts. (28 sts)
Row 9: P1, inc, p7, inc, p18. (30 sts)

Row 10: Inc, k29, cast on 3 sts. (34 sts)
Row 11: Purl.
Cont in fu.
Row 12: [K1, loopy st 1] 16 times, k2, cast on 4 sts, with RS facing k8 from spare needle of Right Back Leg, cast on 2 sts. (48 sts)
Row 13: P12, inc, p8, inc, p8, inc, p17. (51 sts)
Cont in gh.
Row 14: Inc, k50. (52 sts)
Row 15: Purl.
Cont in fu.
Row 16: [K1, loopy st 1] 25 times, k2.
Row 17: Purl.
Cont in gh.
Work 2 rows st st.
Cont in fu.
Row 20: [K1, loopy st 1] 25 times, k2.
Row 21: Purl.
Cont in gh.
Row 22: Inc, k51. (53 sts)
Row 23: Purl.
Cont in fu.
Row 24: K1, [loopy st 1, k1] 26 times.
Row 25: Purl.
Cont in gh.
Row 26: Inc, k52. (54 sts)
Row 27: Purl.
Cont in fu.
Row 28: [K1, loopy st 1], 26 times, k2.
Row 29: Purl.
Cont in gh.
Row 30: Knit.
Row 31: P54, cast on 9 sts. (63 sts)
Join in fu.
Row 32: K10gh, [loopy st 1fu, k1fu] 26 times, k1fu.
Row 33: P53fu, p9gh, incgh. (64 sts)
Cont in gh.
Row 34: Inc, k4, inc, k1, inc, k1, inc, k54. (68 sts)
Row 35: Purl.
Join in fu.

Row 36: K6gh, incgh, k3gh, incgh, k2gh, k1fu, [loopy st 1fu, k1fu] 27 times. (70 sts)
Row 37: P57fu, p13gh.
Row 38: K13gh, loopy st 1fu, k1gh, loopy st 1fu, k24gh, k2toggh, k6gh, k2toggh, k6gh, k2toggh, k12gh. (67 sts)
Row 39: P65gh, p2toggh. (66 sts)
Row 40: Cast (bind) off 3 sts gh, k6gh icos, [loopy st 1fu, k1fu] 11 times, loopy st 1fu, k2togfu, [loopy st 1fu, k1fu] 3 times, loopy st 1fu, k2togfu, [loopy st 1fu, k1fu] 2 times, loopy st 1fu, k2togfu, [loopy st 1fu, k1fu] 7 times, k2togfu. (59 sts)
Row 41: P53fu, p6gh.
Row 42: Cast (bind) off 2 sts gh, k2gh icos, k2toggh, loopy st 1fu, k2toggh, loopy st 1fu, k47gh, k2toggh. (54 sts)
Row 43: Cast (bind) off 37 sts gh, p17gh icos. (17 sts)
Row 44: K2toggh, k1gh, loopy st 1fu, k2toggh, loopy st 1fu, k2toggh, [loopy st 1fu, k1gh] 3 times, k2toggh. (13 sts)
Row 45: Cast (bind) off 4 sts gh, p7gh icos, p2toggh. (8 sts)
Row 46: K2toggh, loopy st 2fu, k2gh, k2toggh. (6 sts)
Row 47: P2toggh, p2gh, p2toggh. (4 sts)
Cast (bind) off.

Left Side of Body and Head

With gh, cast on 2 sts.
Row 1: Knit.
Row 2: [Inc] twice. (4 sts)
Row 3: Knit.
Row 4: Inc, p2, inc. (6 sts)
Row 5: Knit.
Row 6: Inc, p5, with WS facing p7 from spare needle of Left Front Leg, cast on 8 sts. (22 sts)
Row 7: Knit.
Cont in fu.
Row 8: P22, cast on 5 sts. (27 sts)
Row 9: K1, inc, [loopy st 1, k1] 3 times, loopy st 1, inc, [loopy st 1, k1] 8 times, inc. (30 sts)

Cont in gh.
Row 10: Inc, p29, cast on 3 sts. (34 sts)
Row 11: Knit.
Cont in fu.
Row 12: P34, cast on 4 sts, with WS facing p8 from spare needle of Left Back Leg, cast on 2 sts. (48 sts)
Row 13: K2, [loopy st 1, k1] 7 times, inc, [loopy st 1, k1] 3 times, loopy st 1, inc, [loopy st 1, k1] 3 times, loopy st 1, inc, [loopy st 1, k1] 7 times, k1. (51 sts)
Cont in gh.
Row 14: Inc, p50. (52 sts)
Row 15: Knit.
Cont in fu.
Row 16: Purl.
Row 17: [K1, loopy st 1] 25 times, k2.
Cont in gh.
Work 2 rows st st.
Cont in fu.
Row 20: Purl.
Row 21: K1, [k1, loopy st 1] 25 times, k1.
Cont in gh.
Row 22: Purl.
Row 23: Inc, k51. (53 sts)
Cont in fu.
Row 24: Purl.
Row 25: K1, [loopy st 1, k1] 26 times.
Cont in gh.
Row 26: Inc, p52. (54 sts)
Row 27: Knit.
Cont in fu.
Row 28: Purl.
Row 29: [K1, loopy st 1] 26 times, k2.
Cont in gh.
Row 30: Purl.
Row 31: K54, cast on 9 sts. (63 sts)
Join in fu.
Row 32: P10fu, p53gh.
Row 33: [K1fu, loopy st 1fu] 26 times, k1fu, k9gh, incgh. (64 sts)
Cont in gh.
Row 34: Inc, p4, inc, p1, inc, p1, inc, p54. (68 sts)

Row 35: Knit.
Join in fu.
Row 36: P13gh, p55fu.
Row 37: [K1fu, loopy st 1fu] 27 times, k1fu, k2gh, incgh, k3gh, incgh, k6gh. (70 sts)
Row 38: P38gh, p2toggh, p6gh, p2toggh, p6gh, p2toggh, p14gh. (67 sts)
Row 39: K51gh, loopy st 1fu, k1gh, loopy st 1fu, k11gh, k2toggh. (66 sts)
Row 40: Cast (bind) off 3gh sts, p9gh icos, p20fu, p2togfu, p7fu, p2togfu, p5fu, p2togfu, p14fu, p2togfu. (59 sts)
Row 41: [K1fu, loopy st 1fu] 26 times, k1fu, p6gh.
Row 42: Cast (bind) off 2 sts gh, p2gh icos, p2toggh, p1gh, p2toggh, p48gh, p2toggh.

(54 sts)
Row 43: Cast (bind) off 37 sts gh, k2gh icos, [loopy st 1fu, k1gh] 7 times, k1gh. (17 sts)
Row 44: P2toggh, p2gh, p2togfu, p1gh, p2togfu, p6gh, p2togfu. (13 sts)
Row 45: Cast (bind) off 4 sts gh, k4gh icos, loopy st 1fu, k1gh, loopy st 1fu, k2toggh. (8 sts)
Row 46: P2toggh, p4gh, p2toggh. (6 sts)
Row 47: K2toggh, loopy st 2fu, k2toggh. (4 sts)
Cast (bind) off.

Tummy

With gh, cast on 4 sts.
Beg with a k row, work 12 rows st st.

Coat

Cut the loops after sewing up, then comb for a smooth finish.

83

Horns

Manipulate the horns into a big curving sweep.

Row 13: K1, [inc] twice, k1. (6 sts)
Work 33 rows st st.
Row 47: K2tog, k2, k2tog. (4 sts)
Work 2 rows st st.
Row 50: [P2tog] twice. (2 sts)
Cast (bind) off.

Tail

With double-pointed needles and fu, cast on 5 sts.
Work i-cord as folls:
Row 1: Knit.
Row 2: K1, loopy st 3, k1.

Row 3: Knit.
Row 4: K1, loopy st 3, k1.
Cont in gh.
Knit 20 rows.
Cast (bind) off.

Horn

(make 2 the same)
With cl, cast on 5 sts.
Beg with a k row, work 16 rows st st.
Row 17: K2tog, k1, k2tog. (3 sts)
Work 5 rows st st.
Row 23: K3tog and fasten off.

To Make Up

SEWING IN ENDS Sew in ends, leaving ends from cast on and cast (bound) off rows for sewing up.

LEGS With WS together and whip stitch, fold each leg in half and sew up legs on RS, starting at hooves.

HEAD AND BODY Sew from front of front legs, up chest, around head, along back and down bottom.

TUMMY Sew cast on row of tummy to base of cow's bottom (where legs begin), and sew cast (bound) off row to front of front legs. Ease and sew tummy to fit body. Leave a 2.5cm (1in) gap between front and back legs on one side.

STUFFING Pipecleaners are used to stiffen the legs and help bend them into shape. Fold a pipecleaner into a U-shape and measure against front two legs. Cut to fit approximately, leaving an extra 2.5cm (1in) at both ends. Fold these ends over to stop the pipecleaner poking out of the hooves. Roll a little stuffing around pipecleaner and slip into body, one end down each front leg. Repeat with second pipecleaner and back legs. Starting at the head, stuff the cow firmly, but do not stuff flap of skin at front legs, then sew up the gap. Mould body into shape.

TAIL Attach cast (bound) off row of tail to start of bottom.

HORNS Cut two lengths of pipecleaner 2.5cm (1in) longer than horns. Wrap each horn around a pipecleaner so that one end of pipecleaner protrudes and sew up. Push protruding ends of horns into sides of head as in photograph, sew in place and bend into shape.

EYES With ch, sew 3-loop French knots positioned as in photograph.

NOSE With ch, sew 5 long satin stitches horizontally across tip of nose. With cl, sew 3-loop French knots for nostrils.

LOOPS Cut loops and trim.

Llama

The llama is a South American domestic animal
that has recently become very popular in the
UK. If overhandled in their youth, they will grow
up to treat humans as other llamas, spitting,
kicking and neck-wrestling with them. Llamas
also hum as a form of communication. Hilaire
Belloc described them perfectly: 'The llama is a
woolly sort of fleecy hairy goat, with an indolent
expression and an undulating throat; like an
unsuccessful literary man.'

Llama

The llama is made up with the purl side as the right side.

Measurements

Length: 17cm (6¾in)
Height to top of ears: 22cm (8¾in)

Materials

- Pair of 2¾mm (US 2) knitting needles
- Double-pointed 2¾mm (US 2) knitting needles (for holding stitches)
- 20g (¾oz) of Rowan Kidsilk Haze in Mud 652 (mu) used DOUBLE throughout
- 30g (1¼oz) of Rowan Alpaca Cotton in Rice 400 (ri)

NOTE: most of this animal uses 2 strands of mu and 1 strand of ri held together, and this is called muri

- Tiny amount of Rowan Pure Wool 4ply in Black 404 (bl) for eyes and nose
- 2 pipecleaners for legs

Abbreviations

See page 172.
See page 172 for Wrap and Turn Method.

NOTE: work as directed, but to create a llama as in photograph, make up with purl side as right side.

Right Back Leg

With ri, cast on 5 sts.
Beg with a k row, work 14 rows st st.
Join in mu and cont in muri.
Row 15: K1, inc, k1, inc, k1. (7 sts)

Row 16: Purl.
Row 17: K1, inc, k3, inc, k1. (9 sts)
Row 18: Purl.
Row 19: K1, inc, k5, inc, k1. (11 sts)
Row 20: Purl.
Row 21: K1, inc, k7, inc, k1. (13 sts)
Row 22: Purl.
Row 23: K1, inc, k9, inc, k1. (15 sts)
Row 24: Purl.*
Row 25: Cast (bind) off 7 sts, k to end (hold 8 sts on spare needle for Right Side of Body).

Left Back Leg

Work as for Right Back Leg to *.
Row 25: K8, cast (bind) off 7 sts (hold 8 sts on spare needle for Left Side of Body).

Legs

The llama's legs are so slim that they barely need stuffing.

Right Front Leg

With ri, cast on 5 sts.
Beg with a k row, work 18 rows st st.
Join in mu and cont in muri.
Row 19: K1, inc, k1, inc, k1. (7 sts)
Work 3 rows st st.
Row 23: K1, inc, k3, inc, k1. (9 sts)
Row 24: Purl.
Row 25: K1, inc, k2, inc, k2, inc, k1. (12 sts)
Row 26: Purl.**
Row 27: Cast (bind) off 6 sts, k to end (hold 6 sts on spare needle for Right Side of Body).

Left Front Leg

Work as for Right Front Leg to **.
Row 27: K6, cast (bind) off 6 sts (hold 6 sts on spare needle for Left Side of Body).

Right Side of Body

Row 1: With muri, cast on 1 st, with RS facing k6 from spare needle of Right Front Leg, cast on 15 sts, k8 from spare needle of Right Back Leg. (30 sts)
Row 2: Purl.
Row 3: Inc, k29. (31 sts)
Row 4: P2tog, p29. (30 sts)
Row 5: Inc, k29. (31 sts)
Row 6: Purl.
Row 7: Knit.
Row 8: Purl.
Row 9: Inc, k30. (32 sts)
Row 10: Purl.
Row 11: Inc, k31. (33 sts)
Work 3 rows st st.
Row 15: K2tog, k31. (32 sts)
Row 16: Purl.
Row 17: K30, k2tog. (31 sts)
Row 18: P2tog, p29. (30 sts)
Row 19: K2tog, k28. (29 sts)
Row 20: P2tog, p27. (28 sts)
Row 21: K2tog, k24, k2tog. (26 sts)
Cast (bind) off 17 sts, p to end (hold 9 sts on spare needle for Neck and Head).

Left Side of Body

Row 1: With muri, cast on 1 st, with WS facing p6 from spare needle of Left Front Leg, cast on 15 sts, p8 from spare needle of Left Back Leg. (30 sts)
Row 2: Knit.
Row 3: Inc, p29. (31 sts)
Row 4: K2tog, k29. (30 sts)
Row 5: Inc, p29. (31 sts)
Row 6: Knit.
Row 7: Purl.
Row 8: Knit.
Row 9: Inc, p30. (32 sts)
Row 10: Knit.
Row 11: Inc, p31. (33 sts)
Work 3 rows st st.
Row 15: P2tog, p31. (32 sts)
Row 16: Knit.
Row 17: P30, p2tog. (31 sts)
Row 18: K2tog, k29. (30 sts)
Row 19: P2tog, p28. (29 sts)
Row 20: K2tog, k27. (28 sts)
Row 21: P2tog, p24, p2tog. (26 sts)
Cast (bind) off 17 sts, k to end (hold 9 sts on spare needle for Neck and Head).

Neck and Head

Row 1: With muri and RS facing, k9 from spare needle of Right Side of Body, then k9 from spare needle of Left Side of Body. (18 sts)
Work 3 rows st st.
Row 5: K2tog, k14, k2tog. (16 sts)
Row 6: Purl.
Row 7: K2tog, k12, k2tog. (14 sts)
Work 5 rows st st.
Row 13: K2tog, k10, k2tog. (12 sts)
Work 5 rows st st.
Row 19: K10, w&t (leave 2 sts on left-hand needle unworked).
Row 20: Working top of head on centre 8 sts only, p8, w&t.
Row 21: K8, w&t.
Row 22: P8, w&t.

Tail

The llama's tail does not need
to be caught down.

Row 23: K10. (12 sts in total)
Row 24: P1, p2tog, p6, p2tog, p1. (10 sts)
Row 25: K2tog, k5, w&t (leave 3 sts on left-
hand needle unworked).
Row 26: Working top of head on centre 4 sts
only, p4, w&t.
Row 27: K4, w&t.
Row 28: P4, w&t.
Row 29: K5, k2tog. (8 sts in total)
Row 30: Purl.
Row 31: K2tog, k4, k2tog. (6 sts)
Row 32: Purl.
Row 33: K2tog, k2, k2tog. (4 sts)
Row 34: Purl.
Row 35: Knit.
Row 36: Purl.
Cast (bind) off 4 sts.

Tummy

With muri, cast on 1 st.
Beg with a k row, cont in st st.
Row 1: Inc. (2 sts)
Row 2: Purl.
Row 3: [Inc] twice. (4 sts)
Row 4: Purl.
Row 5: Inc, k2, inc. (6 sts)
Work 41 rows st st.
Row 47: K2tog, k2, k2tog. (4 sts)
Work 21 rows st st.
Row 69: K1, k2tog, k1. (3 sts)
Work 23 rows st st.
Cast (bind) off 3 sts.

Tail

With muri, cast on 6 sts.
Beg with a k row, work 6 rows st st.
Row 7: K2tog, k2, k2tog. (4 sts)
Row 8: [P2tog] twice. (2 sts)
Row 9: K2tog and fasten off.

Ear

(make 2 the same)
With muri, cast on 4 sts.
Beg with a k row, work 2 rows st st.

Row 3: K1, k2tog, k1. (3 sts)
Work 4 rows st st.
Row 8: P1, p2tog. (2 sts)
Row 9: K2tog and fasten off.

To Make Up

SEWING IN ENDS Sew in ends, leaving ends from cast on and cast (bound) off rows for sewing up.

LEGS With knit sides together and whip stitch, fold each leg in half and sew up legs, starting at hooves.

BODY Sew along back of llama and 3cm (1¼in) down bottom.

TUMMY Sew cast on row of tummy to where you have finished sewing down bottom, and sew cast (bound) off row to nose. Ease and sew tummy to fit body. Leave a 2.5cm (1in) gap between front and back legs on one side.

STUFFING Pipecleaners are used to stiffen the legs and help bend them into shape. Fold a pipecleaner into a U-shape and measure against front two legs. Cut to fit approximately, leaving an extra 2.5cm (1in) at both ends. Fold these ends over to stop the pipecleaner poking out of the hooves. Roll a little stuffing around pipecleaner and slip into body, one end down each front leg. Repeat with second pipecleaner and back legs. Starting at the head, stuff the llama firmly, then sew up the gap. Mould body into shape.

TAIL With purl side facing outwards, attach cast on row of tail to start of bottom.

EARS With knit side facing forwards, sew cast on row of each ear to top of head, with 1 st between ears.

EYES With bl, sew 2-loop French knots positioned as in photograph.

NOSE With bl, sew 2 sts, both approx 7mm (¼in) long, in a T-shape at tip of nose.

Pig

Pigs occupy a special place in our affections. As Winston Churchill said, 'Dogs look up to us, cats look down on us, but pigs treat us as equals.' It seems immensely unfair that the word 'pig' is used as an insult. One particularly heroic pig event took place in 1998 when the 'Tamworth Two' escaped on the way to an abattoir in Malmesbury. They went on the run for over a week, and when they were finally recaptured and threatened with a return to the abattoir, there was a national outcry and they eventually went to live happily ever after on a rare-breeds farm in Kent.

Pig

This lovely pink pig
is easy to knit.

Measurements
Length: 20cm (8in)
Height to top of head: 9cm (3½in)

Materials
- Pair of 3¼mm (US 3) knitting needles
- Double-pointed 3¼mm (US 3) knitting needles (for holding stitches)
- 25g (1oz) of Rowan Pure Wool DK in Dew 057 (de)
- Tiny amount of Rowan Pure Wool 4ply in Black 404 (bl) for eyes, nose and trotters
- 2 pipecleaners for legs

Abbreviations
See page 172.

Right Back Leg
With de, cast on 4 sts.
Beg with a k row, work 6 rows st st.
Row 7: K1, [inc] twice, k1. (6 sts)
Row 8: Purl.
Row 9: Inc, k4, inc. (8 sts)
Row 10: Purl.**
Row 11: K1, [inc] twice, k2, [inc] twice, k1. (12 sts)
Row 12: Purl.
Row 13: K1, [inc] twice, k6, [inc] twice, k1. (16 sts)
Row 14: Purl.*
Row 15: Cast (bind) off 8 sts, k to end (hold 8 sts on spare needle for Right Side of Body).

Left Back Leg
Work as for Right Back Leg to *.
Row 15: K8, cast (bind) off 8 sts (hold 8 sts on spare needle for Left Side of Body).

Right Front Leg
Work as for Right Back Leg to **.
Row 11: K1, [inc] twice, k2, [inc] twice, k1. (12 sts)
Work 3 rows st st.***
Row 15: Cast (bind) off 6 sts, k to end (hold 6 sts on spare needle for Right Side of Body).

Left Front Leg
Work as for Right Front Leg to ***.
Row 15: K6, cast (bind) off 6 sts (hold 6 sts on spare needle for Left Side of Body).

Right Side of Body and Head
With de, cast on 18 sts.
Row 1: Knit.
Row 2: Inc, p16, inc, with WS facing p6 from spare needle of Right Front Leg. (26 sts)
Row 3: K25, inc, with RS facing k8 from spare needle of Right Back Leg, cast on 1 st. (36 sts)
Row 4: P36, cast on 14 sts. (50 sts)
Row 5: K49, inc. (51 sts)
Row 6: Purl.
Row 7: Cast (bind) off 3 sts, k47 icos, inc. (49 sts)
Row 8: P47, p2tog. (48 sts)
Row 9: K2tog, k45, inc. (48 sts)
Row 10: P46, p2tog. (47 sts)
Row 11: K46, inc. (48 sts)
Row 12: Purl.
Row 13: K2tog, k46. (47 sts)
Row 14: Purl.
Row 15: K2tog, k45. (46 sts)
Row 16: Purl.
Row 17: Cast (bind) off 5 sts, k to end. (41 sts)
Row 18: P39, p2tog. (40 sts)
Row 19: K2tog, k36, k2tog. (38 sts)

Body

The pig is an animal that
needs to be well stuffed.

Row 20: P2tog, p34, p2tog. (36 sts)
Row 21: Cast (bind) off 5 sts, k29 icos,
k2tog. (30 sts)
Row 22: P2tog, p26, p2tog. (28 sts)
Cast (bind) off.

Left Side of Body and Head

With de, cast on 18 sts.
Row 1: Purl.
Row 2: Inc, k16, inc, with RS facing k6 from
spare needle of Left Front Leg. (26 sts)
Row 3: P25, inc, with WS facing p8 from spare
needle Left Back Leg, cast on 1 st. (36 sts)
Row 4: K36, cast on 14 sts. (50 sts)
Row 5: P49, inc. (51 sts)
Row 6: Knit.
Row 7: Cast (bind) off 3 sts, p47 icos, inc.
(49 sts)

Row 8: K47, k2tog. (48 sts)
Row 9: P2tog, p45, inc. (48 sts)
Row 10: K46, k2tog. (47 sts)
Row 11: P46, inc. (48 sts)
Row 12: Knit.
Row 13: P2tog, p46. (47 sts)
Row 14: Knit.
Row 15: P2tog, p45. (46 sts)
Row 16: Knit.
Row 17: Cast (bind) off 5 sts, p to end. (41 sts)
Row 18: K39, k2tog. (40 sts)
Row 19: P2tog, p36, p2tog. (38 sts)
Row 20: K2tog, k34, k2tog. (36 sts)
Row 21: Cast (bind) off 5 sts, p29 icos,
p2tog. (30 sts)
Row 22: K2tog, k26, k2tog. (28 sts)
Cast (bind) off.

Tail

The pig's tail will curl naturally, so simply twist it around into a curl.

Tummy

With de, cast on 1 st.
Beg with a k row, cont in st st.
Row 1: Inc. (2 sts)
Row 2: Purl.
Row 3: [Inc] twice. (4 sts)
Row 4: Purl.
Row 5: Inc, k2, inc. (6 sts)
Row 6: Purl.
Row 7: Inc, k4, inc. (8 sts)
Work 41 rows st st.
Row 49: K2tog, k4, k2tog. (6 sts)
Work 7 rows st st.
Row 57: K2tog, k2, k2tog. (4 sts)
Work 3 rows st st.
Row 61: [K2tog] twice. (2 sts)
Row 62: P2tog and fasten off.

Tail

With de, cast on 20 sts.
Cast (bind) off.

Ear

(make 2 the same)
With de, cast on 5 sts.
Row 1 (forms ridge on RS): Knit.
Row 2: Inc, k3, inc. (7 sts)
Row 3: Purl.
Row 4: K3, inc, k3. (8 sts)
Work 3 rows st st.
Row 8: K2tog, k4, k2tog. (6 sts)
Row 9: Purl.
Row 10: K2tog, k2, k2tog. (4 sts)
Row 11: Purl.
Row 12: [K2tog] twice. (2 sts)
Row 13: P2tog and fasten off.

To Make Up

SEWING IN ENDS Sew in ends, leaving ends from cast on and cast (bound) off rows for sewing up.

LEGS With WS together and whip stitch, fold each leg in half and sew up legs on RS, starting at trotters.

BODY Sew along back of pig and 5cm (2in) down bottom.

TUMMY Sew cast on row of tummy to where you have finished sewing down bottom, and sew cast (bound) off row to nose. Ease and sew tummy to fit body. Leave a 2.5cm (1in) gap between front and back legs on one side.

STUFFING Pipecleaners are used to stiffen the legs and help bend them into shape. Fold a pipecleaner into a U-shape and measure against front two legs. Cut to fit approximately, leaving an extra 2.5cm (1in) at both ends. Fold these ends over to stop the pipecleaner poking out of the trotters. Roll a little stuffing around pipecleaner and slip into body, one end down each front leg. Repeat with second pipecleaner and back legs. Starting at the head, stuff the pig firmly, then sew up the gap. Mould body into shape.

TAIL Attach tail to start of bottom. Twist tail around to curl in a pig-like way.

EARS With knit side uppermost, sew cast on row of each ear to top of head, approx level with centre of front legs and with 3 rows between ears. The ears should flop forwards.

TROTTERS With bl, sew 2 sts vertically down front of each trotter.

EYES With bl, make a tiny horizontal stitch for each eye, 4 rows below centre seam.

NOSTRILS With bl, sew tiny stitches for nostrils.

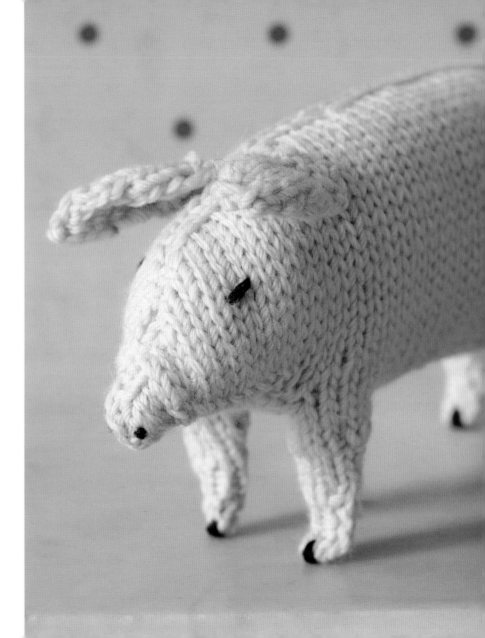

Piglet

We all love piglets. It's hard to decide which is the most beloved of all fictional piglets – Piglet himself, Winnie-the-Pooh's diminutive chum; Babe, the hero of Dick King-Smith's brilliant *The Sheep-Pig* (later made into a wonderful film); or Wilbur, of *Charlotte's Web* fame. There are numerous other examples of fictional piglets, and they're very big on the internet, especially the tiny teacup variety.

Piglet

This is a tiny version of the pig and therefore a good animal to start with.

Measurements
Length: 13cm (5in)
Height to top of head: 6cm (2½in)

Materials
- Pair of 3¼mm (US 3) knitting needles
- Double-pointed 3¼mm (US 3) knitting needles (for holding stitches)
- 25g (1oz) of Rowan Pure Wool DK in Dew 057 (de)
- Tiny amount of Rowan Pure Wool 4ply in Black 404 (bl) for eyes, nose and trotters
- 2 pipecleaners for legs

Abbreviations
See page 172.

Right Back Leg
With de, cast on 4 sts.
Beg with a k row, work 4 rows st st.
Row 5: K1, [inc] twice, k1. (6 sts)
Row 6: Purl.
Row 7: K1, inc, k2, inc, k1. (8 sts)
Row 8: Purl.*
Row 9: Cast (bind) off 4 sts, k to end (hold 4 sts on spare needle for Right Side of Body).

Left Back Leg
Work as for Right Back Leg to *.
Row 9: K4, cast (bind) off 4 sts (hold 4 sts on spare needle for Left Side of Body).

Right Front Leg
With de, cast on 4 sts.
Beg with a k row, work 4 rows st st.
Row 5: K1, [inc] twice, k1. (6 sts)
Work 3 rows st st.**
Row 9: Cast (bind) off 3 sts, k to end (hold 3 sts on spare needle for Right Side of Body).

Left Front Leg
Work as for Right Front Leg to **.
Row 9: K3, cast (bind) off 3 sts (hold 3 sts on spare needle for Left Side of Body).

Right Side of Body and Head
Row 1: With de, cast on 2 sts, with RS facing k3 from spare needle of Right Front Leg, cast on 10 sts, k4 from spare needle of Right Back Leg, cast on 3 sts. (22 sts)
Row 2: Purl.
Row 3: K21, inc. (23 sts)
Row 4: P23, cast on 8 sts. (31 sts)
Row 5: K30, inc. (32 sts)
Row 6: Purl.
Row 7: Cast (bind) off 3 sts, k28 icos, inc. (30 sts)
Row 8: Purl.
Row 9: K2tog, k28. (29 sts)
Row 10: Purl.
Row 11: K2tog, k25, k2tog. (27 sts)
Row 12: P2tog, p23, p2tog. (25 sts)
Row 13: Cast (bind) off 6 sts, k17 icos, k2tog. (18 sts)
Cast (bind) off.

Left Side of Body and Head
Row 1: With de, cast on 2 sts, with WS facing p3 from spare needle of Left Front Leg, cast on 10 sts, k4 from spare needle of Left Back Leg, cast on 3 sts. (22 sts)
Row 2: Knit.
Row 3: P21, inc. (23 sts)
Row 4: K23, cast on 8 sts. (31 sts)
Row 5: P30, inc. (32 sts)
Row 6: Knit.

Row 7: Cast (bind) off 3 sts, p28 icos, inc. (30 sts)
Row 8: Knit.
Row 9: P2tog, p28. (29 sts)
Row 10: Knit.
Row 11: P2tog, p25, p2tog. (27 sts)
Row 12: K2tog, k23, k2tog. (25 sts)
Row 13: Cast (bind) off 6 sts, p17 icos, p2tog. (18 sts)
Cast (bind) off.

Tummy
With de, cast on 1 st.
Beg with a k row, cont in st st.
Row 1: Inc. (2 sts)
Row 2: Purl.
Row 3: [Inc] twice. (4 sts)
Row 4: Purl.
Row 5: Inc, k2, inc. (6 sts)
Work 33 rows st st.
Row 39: K2tog, k2, k2tog. (4 sts)
Work 3 rows st st.
Row 43: [K2tog] twice. (2 sts)
Row 44: Purl.
Row 45: K2tog and fasten off.

Tail
With de, cast on 14 sts.
Cast (bind) off.

Ear
(make 2 the same)
With de, cast on 3 sts.
Row 1 (forms ridge on RS): Knit.
Row 2: Inc, k1, inc. (5 sts)
Row 3: Purl.
Row 4: K2, inc, k2. (6 sts)
Row 5: Purl.
Row 6: Knit.
Row 7: Purl.
Row 8: K2tog, k2, k2tog. (4 sts)
Row 9: [P2tog] twice. (2 sts)
Row 10: K2tog and fasten off.

To Make Up

SEWING IN ENDS Sew in ends, leaving ends from cast on and cast (bound) off rows for sewing up.

LEGS With WS together and whip stitch, fold each leg in half and sew up legs on RS, starting at trotters.

BODY Sew along back of piglet and 2.5cm (1in) down bottom.

TUMMY Sew cast on row of tummy to where you have finished sewing down bottom, and sew cast (bound) off row to nose. Ease and sew tummy to fit body. Leave a 2.5cm (1in) gap between front and back legs on one side.

STUFFING Pipecleaners are used to stiffen the legs and help bend them into shape. Fold a pipecleaner into a U-shape and measure against front two legs. Cut to fit approximately, leaving an extra 2.5cm (1in) at both ends. Fold these ends over to stop the pipecleaner poking out of the trotters. Roll a little stuffing around pipecleaner and slip into body, one end down each front leg. Repeat with second pipecleaner and back legs. Starting at the head, stuff the piglet firmly, then sew up the gap. Mould body into shape.

TAIL Attach tail to start of bottom. Twist tail around to curl in a pig-like way.

EARS With knit side uppermost, sew cast on row of each ear to top of head, parallel to front of front legs, with 3 rows between ears. The ears should flop forwards.

EYES With bl, make a tiny horizontal stitch for each eye, 2 rows below centre seam and approx 5 sts back from nose (or do French knots if you prefer).

TROTTERS With bl, sew 2 sts vertically down front of each trotter.

NOSTRILS With bl, sew tiny sts for nostrils (optional).

Horse

There is an immense affinity between man and horse. For hundreds of years the horse was a working animal; now supplanted by vehicles, they are mainly ridden for enjoyment. There's a wealth of different ways to engage with horses: racing, hacking, dressage, cross-country, hunting, show jumping and carriage racing. My sister Lucy is a keen horsewoman; her connection with her horse is so strong, they seem to be one entity. Famous horses (both real and make-believe) include Champion the Wonder Horse, Black Beauty, My Little Pony, Red Rum, Arkle and poor Shergar, kidnapped by the IRA but never found.

Horse

The horse is a large but simple animal to knit. The rump needs plenty of stuffing.

Measurements

Length: 30cm (12in)
Height to top of head: 21cm (8¼in)

Materials

- Pair of 3¼mm (US 3) knitting needles
- Double-pointed 3¼mm (US 3) knitting needles (for holding stitches)
- Small amount of Rowan Creative Focus Worsted in Charcoal Heather 00402 (ch) for hooves
- 5g (⅛oz) of Rowan Creative Focus Worsted in Natural 00100 (na)
- 40g (1½oz) of Rowan Pure Wool Worsted in Clove 108 (cv)
- 10g (¼oz) of Rowan Creative Focus Worsted in Ebony 00500 (eb)
- 2 pipecleaners for legs
- Crochet hook for mane

Abbreviations

See page 172.
See page 173 for Loopy Stitch, Work 2-finger loopy stitch throughout pattern.
See page 172 for Short Row Patterning.
See page 173 for Scarf Fringe Method.

Right Back Leg

With ch, cast on 13 sts.
Beg with a k row, work 2 rows st st.
Row 3: Inc, k3, k2tog, k1, k2tog, k3, inc.
(13 sts)
Row 4: Inc, p3, p2tog, p1, p2tog, p3, inc.
(13 sts)
Cont in na.
Row 5: K4, k2tog, k1, k2tog, k4. (11 sts)
Row 6: Purl.
Row 7: K1, loopy st 9, k1.
Row 8: Purl.
Row 9: K1, loopy st 2, k2tog, k1, k2tog, loopy st 2, k1. (9 sts)
Row 10: Purl.
Row 11: K1, loopy st 1, k5, loopy st 1, k1.
Row 12: Purl.
Row 13: K1, loopy st 1, k5, loopy st 1, k1.
Row 14: Purl.**
Join in cv.
Row 15: K1cv, k7na, k1cv.

Fetlocks

Trim the loops for fetlocks to the length you prefer.

Row 16: P2cv, p5na, p2cv.
Row 17: K3cv, incna, k1na, incna, k3cv.
(11 sts)
Row 18: P5cv, p1na, p5cv.
Cont in cv.
Row 19: K4, inc, k1, inc, k4. (13 sts)
Row 20: Purl.
Row 21: K5, inc, k1, inc, k5. (15 sts)
Row 22: Purl.
Row 23: K6, inc, k1, inc, k6. (17 sts)
Row 24: Purl.
Row 25: K7, inc, k1, inc, k7. (19 sts)
Work 3 rows st st.
Row 29: K8, inc, k1, inc, k8. (21 sts)
Work 3 rows st st.*
Row 33: Cast (bind) off 10 sts, k to end
(hold 11 sts of spare needle for Right Side
of Body).

Left Back Leg
Work as for Right Back Leg to *.
Row 33: K11, cast (bind) off 10 sts (hold
11 sts on spare needle for Left Side of Body).

Legs
Stuff the horse's legs well
for added muscle.

Mane

This horse has a casual mane, but it could be made neater if you prefer.

Right Front Leg

Work as for Right Back Leg to **.
Work 2 rows st st.
Join in cv.
Row 17: K3na, k3cv, k3na.
Row 18: P2na, p5cv, p2na.
Row 19: Incna, k7cv, incna. (11 sts)
Row 20: P2na, p7cv, p2na.
Cont in cv.
Row 21: Inc, k9, inc. (13 sts)
Row 22: Purl.
Row 23: Inc, k11, inc. (15 sts)
Work 3 rows st st.***
Row 27: Cast (bind) off 7 sts, k to end (hold 8 sts on spare needle for Right Side of Body).

Left Front Leg

Work as for Right Front Leg to ***.
Row 27: K8, cast (bind) off 7 sts (hold 8 sts on spare needle for Left Side of Body).

Right Side of Body

Row 1: With cv, cast on 1 st, with RS facing k8 from spare needle of Right Front Leg, cast on 11 sts. (20 sts)
Row 2: P19, inc. (21 sts)
Row 3: Inc, k10, inc, k7, inc, k1, cast on 4 sts. (28 sts)
Row 4: Purl.
Row 5: Inc, k11, inc, k7, inc, k5, inc, k1, cast on 2 sts. (34 sts)
Row 6: Purl.
Row 7: K34, cast on 1 st, with RS facing k11 from spare needle of Right Back Leg, cast on 2 sts. (48 sts)
Row 8: Purl.
Row 9: Inc, k47. (49 sts)
Row 10: Purl.
Row 11: K39, inc, k4, inc, k3, inc. (52 sts)
Work 3 rows st st.
Row 15: K40, inc, k6, inc, k3, inc. (55 sts)

Work 7 rows st st.
Row 23: K40, k2tog, k6, k2tog, k5. (53 sts)
Row 24: Purl.
Row 25: K15, k2tog, k7, k2tog, k5, k2tog, k20. (50 sts)
Row 26: P2tog, p48. (49 sts)
Row 27: K2tog, k12, k2tog, k7, k2tog, k12, k2tog, k4, k2tog, k4. (44 sts)
Row 28: P2tog, p42. (43 sts)
Row 29: K19, cast (bind) off 12 sts, k10 icos, k2tog (hold 19 sts on spare needle for Row 32).
Row 30: Working on 11 sts, p2tog, p7, p2tog. (9 sts)
Row 31: Cast (bind) off.
Row 32: Rejoin yarn to rem 19 sts, p19.
Row 33: K2tog, k17. (18 sts)
Row 34: Cast (bind) off 2 sts, p to end (hold 16 sts on spare needle for Neck and Head).

Left Side of Body

Row 1: With cv, cast on 1 st, with WS facing p8 from spare needle of Left Front Leg, cast on 11 sts. (20 sts)
Row 2: K19, inc. (21 sts)
Row 3: Inc, p10, inc, p7, inc, p1, cast on 4 sts. (28 sts)
Row 4: Knit.
Row 5: Inc, p11, inc, p7, inc, p5, inc, p1, cast on 2 sts. (34 sts)
Row 6: Knit.
Row 7: P34, cast on 1 st, with WS facing p11 from spare needle of Left Back Leg, cast on 2 sts. (48 sts)
Row 8: Knit.
Row 9: Inc, p47. (49 sts)
Row 10: Knit.
Row 11: P39, inc, p4, inc, p3, inc. (52 sts)
Work 3 rows st st.
Row 15: P40, inc, p6, inc, p3, inc. (55 sts)
Work 7 rows st st.
Row 23: P40, p2tog, p6, p2tog, p5. (53 sts)
Row 24: Knit.
Row 25: P15, p2tog, p7, p2tog, p5, p2tog, p20. (50 sts)
Row 26: K2tog, k48. (49 sts)
Row 27: P2tog, p12, p2tog, p7, p2tog, p12, p2tog, p4, p2tog, p4. (44 sts)
Row 28: K2tog, k42. (43 sts)
Row 29: P19, cast (bind) off 12 sts, p10 icos, p2tog (hold 19 sts on spare needle for Row 32).
Row 30: Working on 11 sts, k2tog, k7, k2tog. (9 sts)
Row 31: Cast (bind) off.
Row 32: Rejoin yarn to rem 19 sts, k19.
Row 33: P2tog, p17. (18 sts)
Row 34: Cast (bind) off 2 sts, k to end (hold 16 sts on spare needle for Neck and Head).

Neck and Head

Row 1: With cv and RS facing, k16 from spare needle of Right Side of Body, then k16 from spare needle of Left Side of Body. (32 sts)
Row 2: P14, [p2tog] twice, p14. (30 sts)
Row 3: Knit.
Row 4: Inc, p12, [p2tog] twice, p12, inc. (30 sts)
Row 5: K8, k2tog, k10, k2tog, k8. (28 sts)
Row 6: P12, [p2tog] twice, p12. (26 sts)
Row 7: Inc, k10, [k2tog] twice, k10, inc. (26 sts)
Row 8: Purl.
Row 9: K11, [k2tog] twice, k10, w&t (leave 1 st on left-hand needle unworked).
Row 10: P22, w&t.
Row 11: K9, [k2tog] twice, k8, w&t.
Row 12: P18, w&t.
Row 13: K17, w&t.
Row 14: P16, w&t.
Row 15: K6, [k2tog] twice, k5, w&t.
Row 16: P12, w&t.
Row 17: K4, [k2tog] twice, k3, w&t.
Row 18: P8, w&t.
Row 19: K9, w&t.
Row 20: P10, w&t.
Row 21: K11, w&t.

Join in na.
Row 22: P5cv, p2na, p5cv, w&t.
Row 23: K5cv, k2na, k6cv, w&t.
Row 24: P5cv, p4na, p5cv, w&t.
Row 25: K5cv, k4na, k6cv, w&t.
Row 26: P6cv, p3na, p7cv, w&t.
Row 27: K7cv, k3na, k7cv. (18 sts in total)
Row 28: Inccv, p7cv, p2na, p7cv, inccv.
(20 sts)
Row 29: K9cv, k2na, k9cv.
Row 30: P5cv, p2togcv, p2cv, p2na, p2cv,
p2togcv, p5cv. (18 sts)
Row 31: K2togcv, k6cv, k2na, k6cv, k2togcv.
(16 sts)
Row 32: P7cv, p2na, p7cv.
Row 33: K3cv, k2togcv, k2cv, k2na, k2cv,
k2togcv, k3cv. (14 sts)
Row 34: P6cv, p2na, p6cv.
Row 35: K2cv, k2togcv, k2cv, k2na, k2cv,
k2togcv, k2cv. (12 sts)
Row 36: P5cv, p2na, p5cv.
Row 37: K5cv, k2na, k5cv.
Row 38: P5cv, p2na, p5cv.
Row 39: K5cv, p1na, p6cv.
Cont in cv.
Row 40: P12.
Row 41: Cast (bind) off 4 sts, k to end. (8 sts)
Row 42: Cast (bind) off 4 sts, p to end. (4 sts)
Work 3 rows st st.
Cast (bind) off.

Tummy
With cv, cast on 6 sts.
Beg with a k row, work 16 rows st st.
Row 17: K1, inc, k2, inc, k1. (8 sts)
Work 23 rows st st.
Row 41: K2tog, k4, k2tog. (6 sts)
Work 27 rows st st.
Row 69: K2tog, k2, k2tog. (4 sts)
Work 7 rows st st.
Row 77: K1, [inc] twice, k1. (6 sts)
Work 5 rows st st.
Row 83: K1, [k2tog] twice, k1. (4 sts)
Work 3 rows st st.

Row 87: [K2tog] twice. (2 sts)
Row 88: [Inc] twice. (4 sts)
Row 89: Knit.
Cast (bind) off.

Ear
(make 2 the same)
With cv, cast on 5 sts.
Beg with a k row, work 6 rows st st.
Row 7: K2tog, k1, k2tog. (3 sts)
Work 2 rows st st.
Row 10: P3tog and fasten off.

To Make Up
SEWING IN ENDS Sew in ends, leaving ends
from cast on and cast (bound) off rows for
sewing up.
LEGS With WS together and whip stitch,

Head
Stuff firmly into the nose so that
the horse has a characteristic
muzzle and cheek shape.

fold each leg in half and sew up legs on RS, starting at hooves.

BODY Sew along back of horse and around bottom.

NOSE Sew centre section of nose to sides of nose, to make a square shape.

TUMMY Sew cast on row of tummy to base of horse's bottom (where legs begin), and sew cast (bound) off row to nose. Ease and sew tummy to fit body. Leave a 2.5cm (1in) gap between front and back legs on one side.

STUFFING Pipecleaners are used to stiffen the legs and help bend them into shape. Fold a pipecleaner into a U-shape and measure against front two legs. Cut to fit approximately, leaving an extra 2.5cm (1in) at both ends. Fold these ends over to stop the pipecleaner poking out of the hooves. Roll a little stuffing around pipecleaner and slip into body, one end down each front leg. Repeat with second pipecleaner and back legs. Starting at the head, stuff the horse firmly, especially at the bottom, then sew up the gap. Mould body into shape.

TAIL Cut twelve 25cm (10in) lengths of eb yarn and fold in half; with another length, knot the yarn together at the fold. Attach knotted end to start of bottom, then trim.

EARS With purl side facing forwards, sew cast on row of each ear to top of head, with 4 sts between ears.

MANE Cut approx twenty 15cm (6in) lengths of eb yarn and use crochet hook and Scarf Fringe Method (see page 173) to attach 2-strand tassels along centre back of neck up to ears. Trim to shape as in photograph.

FORELOCK Cut four 10cm (4in) lengths of eb yarn and attach single-strand tassels between the ears.

EYES With eb, sew 4-loop French knots positioned as in photograph.

NOSTRILS With eb, make 4-loop elongated French knots at tip of nose.

Sheep

Mankind, and particularly the knitting world, has every reason to be grateful to sheep as they provide us with wool. And where would we be without wool? Sheep have an undeserved reputation for being none-too-bright, but recent studies have proved them to be cleverer than rats. They have been described by one research scientist as being 'as intelligent as a slow monkey'. Sheep in Yorkshire have been spotted rolling across a cattle grid, proving their ingenuity.

Sheep

The sheep is a quick and satisfying knit, and requires firm stuffing.

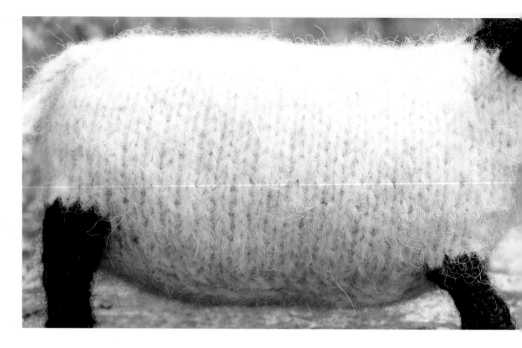

Measurements
Length: 17cm (6¾in)
Height to top of head: 12cm (4¾in)

Materials
- Pair of 2¾mm (US 2) knitting needles
- Double-pointed 2¾mm (US 2) knitting needles (for holding stitches)
- 10g (¼oz) of Rowan Creative Focus Worsted in Ebony 00500 (eb)
- 20g (¾oz) of Rowan Alpaca Cotton in Rice 400 (ri)
- 2 pipecleaners for legs
- 2 tiny black beads for eyes and sewing needle and black thread for sewing on

Abbreviations
See page 172.
See page 172 for Wrap and Turn Method.

Right Back Leg
With eb, cast on 4 sts.
Beg with a k row, work 8 rows st st.
Row 9: K1, [inc] twice, k1.** (6 sts)
Work 3 rows st st.
Row 13: K1, inc, k2, inc, k1. (8 sts)
Row 14: Purl.
Row 15: K1, inc, k4, inc, k1. (10 sts)
Row 16: Purl.*
Row 17: Cast (bind) off 5 sts, k to end (hold 5 sts on spare needle for Right Side of Body).

Left Back Leg
Work as for Right Back Leg to *.
Row 17: K5, cast (bind) off 5 sts (hold 5 sts on spare needle for Left Side of Body).

Right Front Leg
Work as for Right Back Leg to **.
Work 7 rows st st.***
Row 17: Cast (bind) off 3 sts, k to end (hold 3 sts on spare needle for Right Side of Body).

Left Front Leg
Work as for Right Front Leg to ***.
Row 17: K3, cast (bind) off 3 sts (hold 3 sts on spare needle for Left Side of Body).

Body
Stuff the body well. You can get the sheep to stand as you want by manipulating the pipecleaners in the legs.

Right Side of Body

With ri, cast on 16 sts.
Row 1: Inc, k14, inc. (18 sts)
Row 2: P18, with WS facing p3 from spare needle of Right Front Leg. (21 sts)
Row 3: Inc, k20, k5 from spare needle of Right Back Leg. (27 sts)
Row 4: Purl.
Row 5: Inc, k26. (28 sts)
Row 6: Purl.
Row 7: Inc, k26, inc. (30 sts)
Row 8: Purl.
Work 4 rows st st.
Row 13: Inc, k29. (31 sts)
Row 14: Purl.
Work 2 rows st st.
Row 17: Inc, k30. (32 sts)
Row 18: Purl.
Row 19: Knit.
Row 20: P2tog, p30. (31 sts)
Row 21: K29, k2tog. (30 sts)
Row 22: Cast (bind) off 23 sts, p to end (hold 7 sts on spare needle for Neck and Head).

Left Side of Body

With ri, cast on 16 sts.
Row 1: Inc, p14, inc. (18 sts)
Row 2: K18, with RS facing k3 from spare needle of Left Front Leg. (21 sts)
Row 3: Inc, p20, p5 from spare needle of Left Back Leg. (27 sts)
Row 4: Knit.
Row 5: Inc, p26. (28 sts)
Row 6: Knit.
Row 7: Inc, p26, inc. (30 sts)
Row 8: Knit.
Work 4 rows st st.
Row 13: Inc, p29. (31 sts)
Row 14: Knit.
Work 2 rows st st.
Row 17: Inc, p30. (32 sts)
Row 18: Knit.
Row 19: Purl.
Row 20: K2tog, k30. (31 sts)

Row 21: P29, p2tog. (30 sts)
Row 22: Cast (bind) off 23 sts, k to end (hold 7 sts on spare needle for Neck and Head).

Neck and Head

With eb and RS facing, k7 from spare needle of Right Side of Body, then k7 from spare needle of Left Side of Body. (14 sts)
Row 1: P6, p2tog, p6. (13 sts)
Row 2: K2tog, k8, w&t (leave 3 sts on left-hand needle unworked).
Row 3: Working top of head on centre 7 sts only, p7, w&t.
Row 4: K7, w&t.
Row 5: P7, w&t.

Eyes

The sheep has tiny black beads for eyes, which catch the light.

Tail

The sheep's tail hangs down
naturally inwards.

Row 6: K8, k2tog. (11 sts in total)
Row 7: Purl.
Row 8: K8, w&t (leave 3 sts on left-hand
needle unworked).
Row 9: Working top of head on centre 5 sts
only, p5, w&t.
Row 10: K5, w&t.
Row 11: P5, w&t.
Row 12: K8. (11 sts in total)
Row 13: P2tog, p7, p2tog. (9 sts)
Work 4 rows st st.
Row 18: K2tog, k5, k2tog. (7 sts)
Row 19: P2tog, p3, p2tog. (5 sts)
Cast (bind) off 5 sts.

Tummy

With ri, cast on 1 st.
Beg with a p row, cont in st st.
Row 1: Inc. (2 sts)
Row 2: [Inc] twice. (4 sts)
Row 3: Purl.
Row 4: Inc, k2, inc. (6 sts)
Row 5: Purl.
Row 6: Inc, k4, inc. (8 sts)
Work 41 rows st st.
Row 48: K2tog, k4, k2tog. (6 sts)
Work 21 rows st st.
Change to eb.
Work 8 rows st st.
Row 78: K2tog, k2, k2tog. (4 sts)
Row 79: Purl.
Cast (bind) off.

Tail

With ri, cast on 2 sts.
Beg with a k row, work 12 rows st st.
Cast (bind) off.

Ear

(make 2 the same)
With eb, cast on 3 sts.
Beg with a k row, work 4 rows st st.
Row 5: K2tog, k1. (2 sts)
Row 6: P2tog and fasten off.

To Make Up

SEWING IN ENDS Sew in ends, leaving ends from cast on and cast (bound) off rows for sewing up.

LEGS With WS together and whip stitch, fold each leg in half and sew up legs on RS, starting at hooves.

BODY Sew along back of sheep and 4cm (1½in) down bottom.

TUMMY Sew cast on row of tummy to where you have finished sewing down bottom, and sew cast (bound) off row to nose. Ease and sew tummy to fit body. Leave a 2.5cm (1in) gap between front and back legs on one side.

STUFFING Pipecleaners are used to stiffen the legs and help bend them into shape. Fold a pipecleaner into a U-shape and measure against front two legs. Cut to fit approximately, leaving an extra 2.5cm (1in) at both ends. Fold these ends over to stop the pipecleaner poking out of the hooves. Roll a little stuffing around pipecleaner and slip into body, one end down each front leg. Repeat with second pipecleaner and back legs. Starting at the head, stuff the sheep firmly, then sew up the gap. Mould body into shape.

TAIL Attach cast on row of tail to start of bottom.

EARS With purl side facing forwards, sew cast on row of each ear 3 rows from where black of head starts, with 5 sts between ears.

EYES Sew on black beads positioned as in photograph.

Lamb

Adorable, wobbly-legged and vulnerable, lambs
are symbolic of new life, springtime and Easter.
They are equally happy frolicking in the fields
or nestling snugly beside each other.

Lamb

The lamb is easy to knit so it's worth knitting several for your flock.

Measurements
Length: 12cm (4¾in)
Height to top of head: 10cm (4in)

Materials
- Pair of 2¾mm (US 2) knitting needles
- 20g (¾oz) of Rowan Alpaca Cotton in Rice 400 (ri)
- Tiny amount of Rowan Pure Wool 4ply in Black 404 (bl) for eyes
- Tiny amount of Rowan Pure Wool 4ply in Shell 468 (sl) for nose
- 2 pipecleaners for legs
- 2 tiny black beads for eyes and sewing needle and black thread for sewing on

Abbreviations
See page 172.
See page 172 for Wrap and Turn Method.

NOTE: work as directed, but to create a lamb as in photograph, make up with purl side as right side.

Right Back Leg
With ri, cast on 5 sts.
Beg with a k row, work 12 rows st st.**
Row 13: K1, inc, k1, inc, k1. (7 sts)
Row 14: Purl.*
Row 15: Cast (bind) off 3 sts, k to end (hold 4 sts on spare needle for Right Side of Body).

Left Back Leg
Work as for Right Back Leg to *.
Row 15: K4, cast (bind) off 3 sts (hold 4 sts on spare needle for Left Side of Body).

Right Front Leg
Work as for Right Back Leg to **.
Row 13: Cast (bind) off 2 sts, k to end (hold 3 sts on spare needle for Right Side of Body).

Left Front Leg
Work as for Right Back Leg to **.
Row 13: K3, cast (bind) off 2 sts (hold 3 sts on spare needle for Left Side of Body).

Right Side of Body
Row 1: With ri, cast on 1 st, with RS facing k3 from spare needle of Right Front Leg, cast on 7 sts, k4 from spare needle of Right Back Leg. (15 sts)
Row 2: Purl.
Row 3: Knit.

Legs
The lamb has long skinny legs that can be manipulated into any stance you want.

Row 4: P2tog, p13. (14 sts)
Row 5: Inc, k13. (15 sts)
Row 6: Purl.
Row 7: K14, inc. (16 sts)
Row 8: Purl.
Row 9: Inc, k15. (17 sts)
Row 10: Purl.
Row 11: K16, inc. (18 sts)
Row 12: Purl.
Row 13: Inc, k15, k2tog. (18 sts)
Row 14: Cast (bind) off 14 sts, p to end (hold 4 sts on spare needle for Neck and Head).

Left Side of Body

Row 1: With ri, cast on 1 st, with WS facing p3 from spare needle of Left Front Leg, cast on 7 sts, p4 from spare needle of Left Back Leg. (15 sts)
Row 2: Knit.
Row 3: Purl.
Row 4: K2tog, k13. (14 sts)
Row 5: Inc, p13. (15 sts)
Row 6: Knit.
Row 7: P14, inc. (16 sts)
Row 8: Knit.
Row 9: Inc, p15. (17 sts)
Row 10: Knit.
Row 11: P16, inc. (18 sts)
Row 12: Knit.
Row 13: Inc, p15, p2tog. (18 sts)
Row 14: Cast (bind) off 14 sts, k to end (hold 4 sts on spare needle for Neck and Head).

Neck and Head

Row 1: With ri and WS facing, p4 from spare needle of Left Side of Body, then p4 from spare needle of Right Side of Body. (8 sts)
Row 2: Knit.
Row 3: Purl.
Row 4: Inc, k6, w&t (leave 1 st on left-hand needle unworked).
Row 5: Working top of head on centre 6 sts only, p6, w&t.
Row 6: K6, w&t.

Eyes

The lamb has tiny black beads sewn on top of French knots for eyes. The beads are optional but make the lamb even more appealing.

121

Body
The lamb is made up with the purl side as the right side.

Row 7: P6, w&t.
Row 8: K6, inc. (10 sts in total)
Row 9: Purl.
Row 10: K8, w&t (leave 2 sts on left-hand needle unworked).
Row 11: Working top of head on centre 6 sts only, p6, w&t.
Row 12: K6, w&t.
Row 13: P6, w&t.
Row 14: K8. (10 sts in total)
Row 15: P2tog, p6, p2tog. (8 sts)
Row 16: K2tog, k4, k2tog. (6 sts)
Row 17: P2tog, p2, p2tog. (4 sts)
Row 18: [K2tog] twice. (2 sts)
Cast (bind) off.

Tummy
With ri, cast on 1 st.
Beg with a p row, cont in st st.
Row 1: Inc. (2 sts)

Row 2: [Inc] twice. (4 sts)
Row 3: Purl.
Row 4: Inc, k2, inc. (6 sts)
Work 31 rows st st.
Row 36: K2tog, k2, k2tog. (4 sts)
Work 9 rows st st.
Row 46: [K2tog] twice. (2 sts)
Cast (bind) off.

Tail
With ri, cast on 2 sts.
Beg with a k row, work 8 rows st st.
Cast (bind) off.

Ear
(make 2 the same)
With ri, cast on 2 sts.
Beg with a k row, work 4 rows st st.
Cast (bind) off.

To Make Up

SEWING IN ENDS Sew in ends, leaving ends from cast on and cast (bound) off rows for sewing up.

LEGS With knit sides together and whip stitch, fold each leg in half and sew up legs, starting at hooves.

BODY Sew along back of lamb and 2cm (¾in) down bottom.

TUMMY Sew cast on row of tummy to where you have finished sewing down bottom, and sew cast (bound) off row to nose. Ease and sew tummy to fit body. Leave a 2.5cm (1in) gap between front and back legs on one side.

STUFFING Pipecleaners are used to stiffen the legs and help bend them into shape. Fold a pipecleaner into a U-shape and measure against front two legs. Cut to fit approximately, leaving an extra 2.5cm (1in) at both ends. Fold these ends over to stop the pipecleaner poking out of the hooves. Roll a little stuffing around pipecleaner and slip into body, one end down each front leg. Repeat with second pipecleaner and back legs. Starting at the head, stuff the lamb firmly, then sew up the gap. Mould body into shape.

TAIL Attach cast on row of tail to start of bottom.

EARS With knit side facing forwards, sew cast on row of each ear to top of head, with 5 sts between ears.

EYES With bl, sew 2-loop French knots positioned as in photograph. Sew black beads on top of knots.

NOSE With sl, sew 3 satin stitches horizontally across tip of nose.

Ram

Rams are featured in all kinds of unlikely places, from signs of the zodiac (Aries) and Greek mythology (the Golden Fleece) to ghost-ridden pubs. The Ancient Ram Inn at Wotton-under-Edge is reputed to be one of the most haunted pubs in England. Rams are spectacular-looking and have a reputation for virility and leadership. However, rams are not to be trusted and you shouldn't turn your back on them.

Ram

Although he looks dramatic, the ram is no more difficult to knit than the sheep.

Measurements

Length: 18cm (7in)
Height to top of head: 12cm (4¾in)

Materials

- Pair of 2¾mm (US 2) knitting needles
- Double-pointed 2¾mm (US 2) knitting needles (for holding stitches)
- 10g (¼oz) Rowan Creative Focus Worsted in Ebony 00500 (eb)
- 25g (1oz) of Rowan Alpaca Cotton in Rice 400 (ri)
- 5g (⅛oz) of Rowan Pure Wool 4ply in Shale 402 (sh)
- 3 pipecleaners for legs and horns
- 2 tiny black beads for eyes and sewing needle and black thread for sewing on

Abbreviations

See page 172.
See page 172 for Wrap and Turn Method.

Right Back Leg

With eb, cast on 4 sts.
Beg with a k row, work 4 rows st st.
Row 5: K1, [inc] twice, k1. (6 sts)
Work 3 rows st st.
Row 9: K1, inc, k2, inc, k1.** (8 sts)
Row 10: Purl.
Row 11: K1, inc, k4, inc, k1. (10 sts)
Row 12: Purl.*

The Team

The ram, sheep, lamb and sheepdog are part of the same family. Try knitting the whole flock.

Row 13: Cast (bind) off 5 sts, k to end (hold 5 sts on spare needle for Right Side of Body).

Left Back Leg

Work as for Right Back Leg to *.
Row 13: K5, cast (bind) off 5 sts (hold 5 sts on spare needle for Left Side of Body).

Right Front Leg

Work as for Right Back Leg to **.
Work 3 rows st st.***
Row 13: Cast (bind) off 4 sts, k to end (hold 4 sts on spare needle for Right Side of Body).

Left Front Leg

Work as for Right Front Leg to ***.
Row 13: K4, cast (bind) off 4 sts (hold 4 sts on spare needle for Left Side of Body).

Right Side of Body

With ri, cast on 20 sts.
Row 1: Inc, k18, inc. (22 sts)
Row 2: P22, with WS facing p4 from spare needle of Right Front Leg, cast on 3 sts. (29 sts)
Row 3: K29, k5 from spare needle of Right Back Leg. (34 sts)
Row 4: Purl.
Row 5: Inc, k32, inc. (36 sts)
Row 6: Purl.
Row 7: Inc, k34, inc. (38 sts)
Row 8: Purl.
Work 13 rows st st.
Row 22: P2tog, p34, p2tog. (36 sts)
Row 23: Cast (bind) off 5 sts, k29 icos, k2tog. (30 sts)
Row 24: P28, p2tog. (29 sts)
Row 25: K27, k2tog. (28 sts)
Row 26: Cast (bind) off 18 sts, p to end. (10 sts)
Row 27: Knit.
Cast (bind) off.

Left Side of Body

With ri, cast on 20 sts.
Row 1: Inc, p18, inc. (22 sts)
Row 2: K22, with RS facing k4 from spare needle of Left Front Leg, cast on 3 sts. (29 sts)
Row 3: P29, p5 from spare needle of Left Back Leg. (34 sts)
Row 4: Knit.
Row 5: Inc, p32, inc. (36 sts)
Row 6: Knit.
Row 7: Inc, p34, inc. (38 sts)
Row 8: Knit.
Work 13 rows st st.
Row 22: K2tog, k34, k2tog. (36 sts)
Row 23: Cast (bind) off 5 sts, p29 icos, p2tog. (30 sts)
Row 24: K28, k2tog. (29 sts)
Row 25: P27, p2tog. (28 sts)
Row 26: Cast (bind) off 18 sts, k to end. (10 sts)
Row 27: Purl.
Cast (bind) off.

Neck and Head

Row 1: With eb and RS facing, pick up and k10 sts from neck of Right Side of Body, then pick up and k10 sts from neck of Left Side of Body. (20 sts)
Row 2: P9, p2tog, p9. (19 sts)
Row 3: K7, k2tog, k1, k2tog, k7. (17 sts)
Row 4: P6, p2tog, p1, p2tog, p6. (15 sts)
Row 5: K12, w&t (leave 3 sts on left-hand needle unworked).
Row 6: Working top of head on centre 9 sts only, p9, w&t.
Row 7: K9, w&t.
Row 8: P9, w&t.
Row 9: K9, w&t.
Row 10: P9, w&t.
Row 11: K12. (15 sts in total)
Row 12: P2tog, p11, p2tog. (13 sts)
Row 13: K10, w&t (leave 3 sts on left-hand needle unworked).

Body and tail

As for the sheep, stuff the body well and allow the tail to hang naturally.

Row 14: Working top of head on centre 7 sts only, p7, w&t.
Row 15: K7, w&t.
Row 16: P7, w&t.
Row 17: K10. (13 sts in total)
Row 18: P2tog, p9, p2tog. (11 sts)
Row 19: K2tog, k7, k2tog. (9 sts)
Row 20: P2tog, p5, p2tog. (7 sts)
Row 21: K2tog, k3, k2tog. (5 sts)
Cast (bind) off.

Tummy

With ri, cast on 1 st.
Beg with a p row, cont in st st.
Row 1: Inc. (2 sts)
Row 2: [Inc] twice. (4 sts)
Row 3: Purl.
Row 4: Inc, k2, inc. (6 sts)
Row 5: Purl.
Row 6: Inc, k4, inc. (8 sts)
Work 45 rows st st.
Row 52: K2tog, k4, k2tog. (6 sts)
Work 23 rows st st.
Cont in eb.
Work 4 rows st st.
Row 80: K2tog, k2, k2tog. (4 sts)
Work 5 rows st st.
Cast (bind) off.

Tail

With ri, cast on 3 sts.
Beg with a k row, work 14 rows st st.
Cast (bind) off.

Horn

(make 2 the same)
With sh, cast on 4 sts.
Beg with a k row, work 24 rows st st.
Row 25: K1, k2tog, k1. (3 sts)
Work 9 rows st st.
Cast (bind) off.

To Make Up

SEWING IN ENDS Sew in ends, leaving ends from cast on and cast (bound) off rows for sewing up.

LEGS With WS together and whip stitch, fold each leg in half and sew up legs on RS, starting at hooves.

BODY Sew along back of ram and 4.5cm (1¾in) down bottom.

TUMMY Sew cast on row of tummy to where you have finished sewing down bottom, and sew cast (bound) off row to nose. Ease and sew tummy to fit body. Leave a 2.5cm (1in) gap between front and back legs on one side.

STUFFING Pipecleaners are used to stiffen the legs and help bend them into shape. Fold a pipecleaner into a U-shape and measure against front two legs. Cut to fit approximately, leaving an extra 2.5cm (1in) at both ends. Fold these ends over to stop the pipecleaner poking out of the hooves. Roll a little stuffing around pipecleaner and slip into body, one end down each front leg. Repeat with second pipecleaner and back legs. Starting at the head, stuff the ram firmly, then sew up the gap. Mould body into shape.

TAIL Attach cast on row of tail to start of bottom.

HORNS Cut a length of pipecleaner to fit through both horns and thread through head approx 7 rows from where black starts on head. Insert each protruding end of pipecleaner into a horn, then sew horns to head and curl them around as in photograph.

EYES Sew on black beads positioned as in photograph.

Rat

Rats are the stuff of nightmares to many people. Ours is a cuddly knitted farm rat and therefore not at all scary – more Beatrix Potter's Samuel Whiskers than George Orwell's *1984*. Rats have a bad reputation and some fairly disgusting habits, but we kept rats for several years – Max, Mica, Micky, Audrey and Lulu – and they were delightful, particularly Audrey, who was very clever and affectionate and would chirp lovingly in your ear.

Rat

A quick knit, the rat is
knitted in two halves
and then sewn together.

Measurements
Length: 11cm (4½in)
Height to top of head: 6cm (2½in)

Materials
- Pair of 2¾mm (US 2) knitting needles
- Double-pointed 2¾mm (US 2) knitting
  needles (for tail and for holding stitches)
- 20g (¾oz) of Rowan Pure Wool 4ply in
  Shale 402 (sh)
- 10g (¼oz) of Rowan Pure Wool 4ply in
  Shell 468 (sl)
- Tiny amount of Rowan Pure Wool 4ply in
  Black 404 (bl) for eyes and nose
- 2 tiny black beads for eyes and sewing
  needle and black thread for sewing on
- Black thread for whiskers

Abbreviations
See page 172.
See page 172 for I-cord Technique.

Right Side of Body and Head
With sh, cast on 12 sts.
Beg with a k row, work 4 rows st st.
Row 5: K10, inc, k1. (13 sts)
Row 6: Purl.
Row 7: K11, inc, k1. (14 sts)
Row 8: Purl.
Row 9: K12, inc, k1. (15 sts)
Row 10: Purl.
Row 11: Inc, k12, inc, k1. (17 sts)

Tail and Feet
The rat has a long pink tail and
feet, which help him to balance.

Row 12: Purl.
Row 13: K15, inc, k1. (18 sts)
Row 14: Purl.
Row 15: K16, inc, k1. (19 sts)
Row 16: P19, cast on 9 sts. (28 sts)
Row 17: Knit.
Row 18: Purl.
Row 19: K2tog, k26. (27 sts)
Row 20: Purl.
Row 21: K2tog, k25. (26 sts)
Row 22: Purl.
Row 23: K2tog, k24. (25 sts)
Row 24: P2tog, p15, turn and work on these 16 sts only to shape back.
Row 25: K2tog, k12, k2tog. (14 sts)
Row 26: Purl.
Row 27: K2tog, k10, k2tog. (12 sts)
Row 28: Purl.
Cast (bind) off 12 sts.
Rejoin yarn to rem 8 sts to shape head.
Row 24: P2tog, p4, p2tog. (6 sts)
Row 25: K2tog, k4. (5 sts)
Cast (bind) off.

Left Side of Body and Head

With sh, cast on 12 sts.
Beg with a k row, work 4 rows st st.
Row 5: K1, inc, k10. (13 sts)
Row 6: Purl.
Row 7: K1, inc, k11. (14 sts)
Row 8: Purl.
Row 9: K1, inc, k12. (15 sts)
Row 10: Purl.
Row 11: K1, inc, k12, inc. (17 sts)
Row 12: Purl.
Row 13: K1, inc, k15. (18 sts)
Row 14: Purl.
Row 15: K1, inc, k16. (19 sts)
Row 16: Cast on 9 sts, p to end. (28 sts)
Row 17: Knit.
Row 18: Purl.
Row 19: K26, k2tog. (27 sts)
Row 20: Purl.
Row 21: K25, k2tog. (26 sts)

Body
The rat is sitting on his haunches with his front paws raised.

Head
The rat has a sweet and benign expression.

Row 22: Purl.
Row 23: K24, k2tog. (25 sts)
Row 24: P2tog, p4, p2tog, turn and work on these 6 sts only to shape back.
Row 25: K4, k2tog. (5 sts)
Cast (bind) off 5 sts.
Rejoin yarn to rem 17 sts to shape head.
Row 24: P15, p2tog. (16 sts)
Row 25: K2tog, k12, k2tog. (14 sts)
Row 26: Purl.
Row 27: K2tog, k10, k2tog. (12 sts)
Row 28: Purl.
Cast (bind) off 12 sts.

Front Paws
(make 2 the same)
With sl, cast on 4 sts.
Beg with a k row, work 4 rows st st.
Cast (bind) off.

Back Paws
(make 2 the same)
With sl, cast on 5 sts.
Beg with a k row, work 6 rows st st.
Row 7: K1, k2tog, k2. (4 sts)
Row 8: Purl.
Cast (bind) off.

Front of Ear
(make 2 the same)
With sl, cast on 2 sts.
Beg with a k row, cont in st st.
Row 1: [Inc] twice. (4 sts)
Row 2: Purl.
Row 3: Knit.
Cast (bind) off.

Back of Ear
(make 2 the same)
With sl, cast on 3 sts.
Row 1: Inc, k1, inc. (5 sts)
Row 2: Purl.
Row 3: Knit.
Row 4: Purl.
Cast (bind) off.

Tail
With double-pointed needles and sl, cast on 4 sts.
Work i-cord as folls:
Knit 12 rows.
Row 13: K1, k2tog, k1. (3 sts)
Knit 28 rows.
Row 42: K2tog, k1. (2 sts)
Knit 4 rows.
Row 47: K2tog and fasten off.

To Make Up

SEWING IN ENDS Sew in ends, leaving ends from cast on and cast (bound) off rows for sewing up.

BODY With WS together and using whip stitch, sew two sides of rat together, leaving a 2.5cm (1in) gap.

STUFFING Starting at the head, stuff the rat firmly, then sew up the gap. Mould body into shape.

BACK PAWS Sew along lower edge of body, parallel with each other and with 2 rows between paws.

FRONT PAWS Sew at front of body, 8 rows above lower edge and with 2 sts between paws.

TAIL Attach cast on row of tail to bottom just behind back paws.

EARS Sew ear fronts to backs with WS of front facing RS of back. Attach ears to top of head, with 4 rows between ears.

EYES With bl, sew 2-loop French knots positioned as in photograph. Sew black beads on top of knots.

NOSE With bl, sew 3 satin stitches horizontally across tip of nose.

WHISKERS Cut four 8cm (3in) lengths of black thread. Thread these through cheeks, then trim.

Saddleback Pig

The saddleback is a crossbreed of Neapolitan and Essex pigs, a combination that gives it the characteristics of hardiness and excellent mothering skills. Charles Kingsley described it as 'a pig of self-helpful and serene spirit'. Intensive pig farming has meant that the saddleback has become quite rare – there are fewer than 500 breeding sows registered in the UK. Dick King-Smith wrote a lovely book called *Saddlebottom* starring a saddleback pig family.

Saddleback Pig

The saddleback is no more complicated to knit than the single-colour pig.

Measurements

Length: 24cm (9½in)
Height to centre back: 12cm (4¾in)

Materials

- Pair of 3¼mm (US 3) knitting needles
- Double-pointed 3¼mm (US 3) knitting needles (for holding stitches)
- 40g (1½oz) Rowan Creative Focus Worsted in Ebony 00500 (eb)
- 15g (½oz) Rowan Pure Wool DK in Dew 057 (de)
- 2 pipecleaners for legs
- 2 tiny black beads for eyes and sewing needle and black thread for sewing on

Abbreviations

See page 172.

Right Back Leg

With eb, cast on 3 sts.
Beg with a k row, work 4 rows st st.
Row 5: K1, inc, k1.** (4 sts)
Work 5 rows st st.
Row 11: Inc, k2, inc. (6 sts)
Row 12: Purl.
Row 13: Inc, k4, inc. (8 sts)
Row 14: Purl.*
Row 15: Cast (bind) off 4 sts, k to end (hold 4 sts on spare needle for Right Side of Body).

Left Back Leg

Work as for Right Back Leg to *.
Row 15: K4, cast (bind) off 4 sts (hold 4 sts on spare needle for Left Side of Body).

Right Front Leg

With de, work as for Right Back Leg to **.
Work 1 row st st.
Row 7: Inc, k2, inc. (6 sts)
Work 3 rows st st.
Row 11: Inc, k4, inc. (8 sts)
Row 12: Purl.
Row 13: Inc, k6, inc. (10 sts)
Row 14: Purl.***
Row 15: Cast (bind) off 5 sts, k to end (hold 5 sts on spare needle for Right Side of Body).

Left Front Leg

Work as for Right Front Leg to ***.
Row 15: K5, cast (bind) off 5 sts (hold 5 sts on spare needle for Left Side of Body).

Right Side of Body and Head

With eb, cast on 22 sts.
Row 1: Knit.
Row 2: Inc, p20, inc, with de and WS facing p5 from spare needle of Right Front Leg. (29 sts)
Row 3: K5de, k23eb, inceb, with RS facing k4eb from spare needle of Right Back Leg, cast on 1 st. (35 sts)
Row 4: P30eb, p5de, cast on 20 sts eb. (55 sts)
Row 5: K20eb, k5de, k29eb, inceb. (56 sts)
Row 6: P31eb, p5de, p20eb.
Row 7: Cast (bind) off 2 sts eb, k18eb icos, k6de, k29eb, inceb. (55 sts)
Row 8: P31eb, p6de, p16eb, p2togeb. (54 sts)
Row 9: K2togeb, k15eb, k6de, k30eb, inceb. (54 sts)
Row 10: P32eb, p6de, p14eb, p2togeb. (53 sts)
Row 11: K2togeb, k13eb, k6de, k31eb, inceb. (53 sts)

Trotters

The saddleback pig has a single stitch through each hoof to give it trotters.

Row 12: P33eb, p6de, p14eb.
Row 13: K2togeb, k12eb, k6de, k33eb.
(52 sts)
Row 14: P33eb, p6de, p11eb, p2togeb.
(51 sts)
Row 15: K12eb, k7de, k32eb.
Row 16: P32eb, p7de, p12eb.
Row 17: Cast (bind) off 5 sts eb, k7eb icos, k7de, k32eb. (46 sts)
Row 18: P32eb, p7de, p7eb.
Row 19: K2togeb, k5eb, k7de, k32eb.
(45 sts)
Row 20: P32eb, p7de, p6eb.
Row 21: Cast (bind) off 6 sts eb, k1eb icos, k6de, k30eb, k2togeb. (38 sts)
Row 22: P2togeb, p29eb, p7de. (37 sts)
Row 23: Cast (bind) off 7 sts de, k1de icos, k29eb. (30 sts)
Cont in eb.
Row 24: P2tog, p26, p2tog. (28 sts)
Row 25: K2tog, k24, k2tog. (26 sts)
Row 26: P2tog, p22, p2tog. (24 sts)
Cast (bind) off.

Left Side of Body and Head

With eb, cast on 22 sts.
Row 1: Purl.
Row 2: Inc, k20, inc, with de and RS facing k5 from spare needle of Left Front Leg.
(29 sts)
Row 3: P5de, p23eb, inceb, with WS facing p4eb from spare needle of Left Back Leg, cast on 1 st. (35 sts)
Row 4: K30eb, k5de, cast on 20 sts eb.
(55 sts)
Row 5: P20eb, p5de, p29eb, inceb. (56 sts)
Row 6: K31eb, k5de, k20eb.
Row 7: Cast (bind) off 2 sts eb, p18eb icos, p6de, p29eb, inceb. (55 sts)
Row 8: K31eb, k6de, k16eb, k2togeb. (54 sts)
Row 9: P2togeb, p15eb, k6de, k30eb, inceb.
(54 sts)
Row 10: K32eb, k6de, k14eb, k2togeb.
(53 sts)

Row 11: P2togeb, p13eb, p6de, p31eb, inceb.
(53 sts)
Row 12: K33eb, k6de, k14eb.
Row 13: P2togeb, p12eb, p6de, p33eb.
(52 sts)
Row 14: K33eb, k6de, k11eb, k2togeb.
(51 sts)
Row 15: P12eb, p7de, p32eb.
Row 16: K32eb, k7de, k12eb.
Row 17: Cast (bind) off 5 sts eb, p7eb icos, p7de, p32eb. (46 sts)
Row 18: K32eb, k7de, k7eb.
Row 19: P2togeb, p5eb, p7de, p32eb. (45 sts)
Row 20: K32eb, k7de, k6eb.
Row 21: Cast (bind) off 6 sts eb, p1eb icos, p6de, p30eb, p2togeb. (38 sts)

Body
Stuff the saddleback firmly as he's quite a large pig.

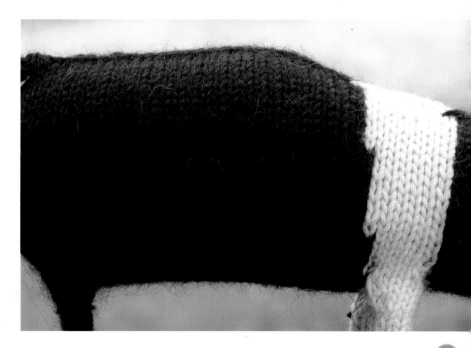

Row 22: K2togeb, k29eb, k7de. (37 sts)
Row 23: Cast (bind) off 7 sts de, p1de icos, p29eb. (30 sts)
Cont in eb.
Row 24: K2tog, k26, k2tog. (28 sts)
Row 25: P2tog, p24, p2tog. (26 sts)
Row 26: K2tog, k22, k2tog. (24 sts)
Cast (bind) off.

Tail

The saddleback's tail will curl naturally, but you can twist it around to help.

Tummy

With eb, cast on 1 st.
Beg with a k row, cont in st st.
Row 1: Inc. (2 sts)

Row 2: Purl.
Row 3: [Inc] twice. (4 sts)
Row 4: Purl.
Row 5: Inc, k2, inc. (6 sts)
Row 6: Purl.
Row 7: Inc, k4, inc. (8 sts)
Work 33 rows st st.
Join in de.
Work 8 rows st st in de.
Work 8 rows st st in eb.
Cont in eb.
Row 57: K2tog, k4, k2tog. (6 sts)
Row 58: Purl.
Work 4 rows st st.
Row 63: K2tog, k2, k2tog. (4 sts)
Row 64: Purl.
Row 65: [K2tog] twice. (2 sts)
Row 66: P2tog and fasten off.

Tail

With eb, cast on 20 sts.
Beg with a k row, work 1 row st st.
Cast (bind) off.

Ears

(make 2 the same)
With eb, cast on 9 sts.
Beg with a k row, work 2 rows st st.
Row 3 (forms ridge on RS): Purl.
Row 4: Purl.
Row 5: K2tog, k5, k2tog. (7 sts)
Work 3 rows st st.
Row 9: K2tog, k3, k2tog. (5 sts)
Work 3 rows st st.
Row 13: K2tog, k1, k2tog. (3 sts)
Row 14: Purl.
Row 15: K2tog, k1. (2 sts)
Row 16: P2tog and fasten off.

To Make Up

SEWING IN ENDS Sew in ends, leaving ends from cast on and cast (bound) off rows for sewing up.

LEGS With WS together and whip stitch, fold each leg in half and sew up legs on RS, starting at trotters.

BODY Sew along back of pig and 6cm (2½in) down bottom.

TUMMY Sew cast on row of tummy to where you have finished sewing down bottom, and sew cast (bound) off row to nose. Ease and sew tummy to fit body, matching pink sections. Leave a 2.5cm (1in) gap between front and back legs on one side.

STUFFING Pipecleaners are used to stiffen the legs and help bend them into shape. Fold a pipecleaner into a U-shape and measure against front two legs. Cut to fit approximately, leaving an extra 2.5cm (1in) at both ends. Fold these ends over to stop the pipecleaner poking out of the trotters. Roll a little stuffing around pipecleaner and slip into body, one end down each front leg. Repeat with second pipecleaner and back legs. Starting at the head, stuff the pig firmly, then sew up the gap. Mould body into shape.

TAIL Attach cast on row of tail to start of bottom. Twist tail around to curl in a pig-like way.

EARS With knit side uppermost, sew cast on row of each ear to top of head at a slight angle, with 2 rows between ears at front and 12 at back, and back of ears starting 3 sts in front of pink section. The ears should flop forwards.

TROTTERS With eb, sew 2 sts vertically down front of front trotters.

EYES Sew on black beads positioned as in photograph.

Silkie

Eccentric-looking, fluffy silkies make excellent
pets for children and can be hand-fed. They are
natural nurturers and are great broody mothers,
so don't expect many eggs. It is thought that the
silkie originated in China. Marco Polo wrote
about them as early as the 1400s, describing
chickens with fur-like feathers. Uniquely, the
silkie has black skin. In Southeast Asia they are
considered to be a delicacy. Silkies have five claws,
but due to insurmountable technical difficulties,
ours has only three.

Silkie

Fluffy and adorable, the silkie is an unusual bird.

Measurements
Length: 10cm (4in)
Height to top of head: 9cm (3½in)

Materials
- Pair of 2¾mm (US 2) knitting needles
- Double-pointed 2¾mm (US 2) knitting needles (for holding stitches)
- 15g (½oz) of Rowan Kidsilk Haze in Cream 634 (cr) used DOUBLE throughout
- 5g (⅙oz) of Rowan Pure Wool 4ply in Black 404 (bl)
- Tiny amount of Rowan Pure Wool 4ply in Eau de Nil 450 (ea) for eyes
- 2 pipecleaners for legs
- 2 tiny black beads for eyes and sewing needle and black thread for sewing on

Abbreviations
See page 172.
See page 173 for Loopy Stitch. Work 2-finger loopy stitch throughout pattern.
See page 172 for Wrap and Turn Method.
See page 173 for Leg and Claw Method.

Right Side of Body
With cr, cast on 10 sts.
Beg with a k row, work 2 rows st st.
Row 3: Inc, k9, cast on 3 sts. (14 sts)
Row 4: Inc, p12, inc. (16 sts)
Row 5: Inc, k15, cast on 2 sts. (19 sts)
Row 6: Inc, p17, inc. (21 sts)
Row 7: Inc, k20. (22 sts)
Row 8: Purl.
Row 9: Inc, k21. (23 sts)
Row 10: Purl.
Row 11: Inc, k20, k2tog. (23 sts)
Row 12: P2tog, p21. (22 sts)
Row 13: Inc, k19, k2tog. (22 sts)
Row 14: Purl.
Row 15: K20, loopy st 1, inc. (23 sts)
Row 16: Purl.
Row 17: Inc, k18, loopy st 1, k1, loopy st 1, k1. (24 sts)
Row 18: Purl.
Row 19: K19, loopy st 1, k1, loopy st 1, k1, inc. (25 sts)
Row 20: Purl.
Row 21: Inc, k17, loopy st 1, k1, loopy st 1, k1, loopy st 1, k2. (26 sts)
Row 22: Purl.
Row 23: K2tog, k16, [loopy st 1, k1] 4 times. (25 sts)
Row 24: Purl.
Row 25: K2tog, k14, [loopy st 1, k1] 4 times, k1. (24 sts)
Row 26: P7, cast (bind) off 3 sts, p12 icos, p2tog (hold 13 sts on spare needle for Neck and Head).
Row 27: Rejoin yarn to rem 7 sts for tail, [k1, loopy st 1] 3 times, inc. (8 sts)
Row 28: Inc, p5, p2tog. (8 sts)
Row 29: Cast (bind) off 2 sts, k1 icos, loopy st 1, k1, loopy st 1, k2. (6 sts)
Cast (bind) off.

Left Side of Body
With cr, cast on 10 sts.
Beg with a p row, work 2 rows st st.
Row 3: Inc, p9, cast on 3 sts. (14 sts)
Row 4: Inc, k12, inc. (16 sts)
Row 5: Inc, p15, cast on 2 sts. (19 sts)
Row 6: Inc, k17, inc. (21 sts)
Row 7: Inc, p20. (22 sts)
Row 8: Knit.
Row 9: Inc, p21. (23 sts)
Row 10: Knit.
Row 11: Inc, p20, p2tog. (23 sts)

Row 12: K2tog, k21. (22 sts)
Row 13: Inc, p19, p2tog. (22 sts)
Row 14: Knit.
Row 15: Purl.
Row 16: Inc, loopy st 1, k20. (23 sts)
Row 17: Purl.
Row 18: K1, loopy st 1, k1, loopy st 1, k18, inc. (24 sts)
Row 19: Purl.
Row 20: Inc, k1, loopy st 1, k1, loopy st 1, k19. (25 sts)
Row 21: Purl.
Row 22: K2, loopy st 1, k1, loopy st 1, k1, loopy st 1, k17, inc. (26 sts)
Row 23: Purl.
Row 24: [K1, loopy st 1] 4 times, k16, k2tog. (25 sts)
Row 25: P23, p2tog. (24 sts)
Row 26: [K1, loopy st 1] 3 times, k1, cast (bind) off 3 sts, k12 icos, k2tog (hold 13 sts on spare needle for Neck and Head).
Row 27: Rejoin yarn to rem 7 sts for tail, p6, inc. (8 sts)
Row 28: Inc, [loopy st 1, k1] twice, loopy st 1, k2tog. (8 sts)
Row 29: Cast (bind) off 2 sts, p to end. (6 sts)
Cast (bind) off.

Body
This is a delicate bird so it only needs light stuffing.

147

Neck and Head

Row 1: With cr and RS facing, k13 from spare needle of Right Side of Body then k13 from spare needle of Left Side of Body. (26 sts)

Row 2: P2tog, p9, [p2tog] twice, p9, p2tog. (22 sts)

Row 3: K2tog, k18, k2tog. (20 sts)

Row 4: P2tog, p6, [p2tog] twice, p6, p2tog. (16 sts)

Join in bl.

Row 5: Cast on 3 sts bl, k2bl, k3cr, loopy st 1cr, [k2togcr] twice, loopy st 1cr, k3cr, k2bl, cast on 3 sts bl. (20 sts)

Row 6: Cast (bind) off 2 sts bl, p4bl icos, p8cr, p6bl. (18 sts)

Row 7: Cast (bind) off 2 sts bl, k5bl, [k1cr, loopy st 1cr] 3 times, w&t (leave 5 sts on left-hand needle unworked).

Row 8: Working top of head on centre 6 sts only, p6cr, w&t.

Row 9: [K1cr, loopy st 1cr] 3 times, w&t.

Row 10: P6cr, w&t.

Row 11: [Loopy st 1cr, k1] 3 times, k2cr, k3bl. (16 sts in total)

Row 12: P2togbl, p1bl, p3cr, [p2togcr] twice, p3cr, p1bl, p2togbl. (12 sts)

Row 13: K2togbl, [k1cr, loopy st 1cr] 4 times, k2togbl. (10 sts)

Cont in cr.

Row 14: P2tog, p1, [p2tog] twice, p1, p2tog. (6 sts)

Cast (bind) off.

Leg and One Front Claw

(make 2 the same)

With bl, cast on 5 sts.

Beg with a k row, work 4 rows st st.

Join in cr.

Row 5: Loopy st 5cr.

Cont in bl.

Work 9 rows st st.

Cast (bind) off.

Front and Back Claws

(make 2 the same)

With bl, cast on 5 sts.

Beg with a k row, work 11 rows st st.

Cast (bind) off.

To Make Up

SEWING IN ENDS Sew in ends, leaving ends from cast on and cast (bound) off rows for sewing up.

BODY With WS together and whip stitch, sew around the body, leaving a 2.5cm (1in) gap.

STUFFING Stuff the silkie firmly (but do not stuff the beak), then sew up the gap. Mould body into shape.

LEGS AND FEET Using a 20cm (8in) length of pipecleaner and the Leg and Claw Method (see page 173), make up legs and feet. The silkie's legs are 2cm (¾in) high. To attach the legs, push protruding ends of pipecleaners into base of body approx 4 rows apart.

EYES Sew black beads a little behind the beak. With ea, sew 2 slanting satin stitches on edge of black section of head.

Claws
The claws work as a tripod
to make the silkie stand.

Turkey

As well as being very odd-looking, turkeys have many unique characteristics. They can run at up to 25mph and fly at up to 55mph; their gender can be ascertained from their droppings, which are different shapes; and they blush when excited or agitated. Benjamin Franklin thought that the turkey should be the national bird of the United States instead of the bald eagle, which he considered 'a bird of bad moral character'.

Turkey

Complicated to knit but worth the effort, the turkey is a dramatic bird.

Measurements
Length: 16cm (6¼in)
Height to top of head: 20cm (8in)

Materials
- Pair of 3¼mm (US 3) knitting needles
- Double-pointed 3¼mm (US 3) knitting needles (for holding stitches)
- 20g (¾oz) of Rowan Felted Tweed DK in Treacle 145 (tr)
- 20g (¾oz) of Rowan Felted Tweed DK in Phantom 153 (ph)
- 15g (½oz) of Rowan Pure Wool DK in Clay 048 (cl)
- 5g (⅛oz) of Rowan Pure Wool DK in Raspberry 028 (ra)
- Tiny amount of Rowan Pure Wool DK in Cloud 058 (cd) for embroidery on head
- 2 pipecleaners for legs and feet
- 2 cocktail sticks or wooden kebab sticks to strengthen legs (if necessary)
- 2 tiny black beads for eyes and sewing needle and black thread for sewing on

Abbreviations
See page 172.
See page 172 for Wrap and Turn Method.
See page 173 for Leg and Claw Method.

Right Side of Body
With tr, cast on 14 sts.
Beg with a k row, work 2 rows st st.
Row 3: Inc, k13. (15 sts)
Row 4: P14, inc. (16 sts)
Row 5: Inc, k14, inc. (18 sts)
Row 6: P17, inc. (19 sts)
Row 7: Inc, k18. (20 sts)
Row 8: P19, inc. (21 sts)
Row 9: Inc, k19, inc. (23 sts)
Row 10: P22, inc. (24 sts)
Row 11: Inc, k23. (25 sts)
Row 12: P24, inc. (26 sts)
Row 13: Inc, k24, inc. (28 sts)
Row 14: P27, inc. (29 sts)
Work 6 rows st st.
Row 21: Inc, k27, inc. (31 sts)
Row 22: Purl.
Row 23: K29, k2tog. (30 sts)
Row 24: P28, p2tog. (29 sts)
Row 25: K2tog, k27. (28 sts)
Row 26: P26, p2tog. (27 sts)
Row 27: K2tog, k23, k2tog. (25 sts)
Row 28: P23, p2tog. (24 sts)
Row 29: K2tog, k22. (23 sts)
Row 30: P21, p2tog. (22 sts)
Row 31: K2tog, k6 (hold these 7 sts on spare needle for Neck and Head), k2tog, k12. (13 sts)
Row 32: P2tog, p9, p2tog. (11 sts)
Row 33: K2tog, k9. (10 sts)
Row 34: P8, p2tog. (9 sts)
Cast (bind) off.

Left Side of Body
With tr, cast on 14 sts.
Beg with a p row, work 2 rows st st.
Row 3: Inc, p13. (15 sts)
Row 4: K14, inc. (16 sts)
Row 5: Inc, p14, inc. (18 sts)
Row 6: K17, inc. (19 sts)
Row 7: Inc, p18. (20 sts)
Row 8: K19, inc. (21 sts)
Row 9: Inc, p19, inc. (23 sts)

Row 10: K22, inc. (24 sts)
Row 11: Inc, p23. (25 sts)
Row 12: K24, inc. (26 sts)
Row 13: Inc, p24, inc. (28 sts)
Row 14: K27, inc. (29 sts)
Work 6 rows st st.
Row 21: Inc, p27, inc. (31 sts)
Row 22: Knit.
Row 23: P29, p2tog. (30 sts)
Row 24: K28, k2tog. (29 sts)
Row 25: P2tog, p27. (28 sts)
Row 26: K26, k2tog. (27 sts)
Row 27: P2tog, p23, p2tog. (25 sts)
Row 28: K23, k2tog. (24 sts)
Row 29: P2tog, p22. (23 sts)
Row 30: K21, k2tog. (22 sts)
Row 31: P2tog, p6 (hold these 7 sts on spare needle for Neck and Head), p2tog, p12. (13 sts)
Row 32: K2tog, k9, k2tog. (11 sts)
Row 33: P2tog, p9. (10 sts)
Row 34: K8, k2tog. (9 sts)
Cast (bind) off.

Tail

With ph, cast on 10 sts.
Beg with a k row, work 2 rows st st.
Row 3: Inc, k2, inc, k2, inc, k2, inc. (14 sts)
Row 4: Purl.
Row 5: Inc, k3, inc, k4, inc, k3, inc. (18 sts)
Row 6: Purl.
Row 7: Inc, k3, inc, k2, inc, k2, inc, k2, inc, k3, inc. (24 sts)
Row 8: Purl.

Tail

The turkey's tail will curl outwards of its own accord as it's knitted in rib and increased.

Eyes

You can use satin stitches or Swiss darning for the eyes, with tiny black beads on top.

Row 9: [K2, p2] to end.
Row 10: Inc, k1, [p2, k2] to last 2 sts, p1, inc. (26 sts)
Row 11: Inc, [k2, p2], to last st, inc. (28 sts)
Row 12: [P2, k2] to end.
Row 13: Inc, p1, [k2, p2] to last 2 sts, k1, inc. (30 sts)
Row 14: K1, [p2, k2] to last st, p1.
Cont in cl.
Row 15: Inc, [p2, k2] to last st, inc. (32 sts)
Row 16: [K2, p2] to end.
Cont in ph.
Row 17: Inc, k1, [p2, k2] to last 2 sts, p1, inc. (34 sts)
Row 18: P1, [k2, p2] to last st, k1.
Row 19: Inc, [k2, p2], to last st, inc. (36 sts)
Row 20: [P2, k2] to end.
Cont in cl.
Row 21: Inc, p1, [k2, p2], to last 2 sts, k1, inc. (38 sts)
Row 22: K1, [p2, k2] to last st, p1.
Cont in ph.
Row 23: Inc, [p2, k2] to last st, inc. (40 sts)
Row 24: [K2, p2] to end.
Row 25: Inc, k1, [p2, k2] to last 2 sts, p1, inc. (42 sts)
Row 26: P1, [k2, p2] to last st, k1.
Row 27: Inc, [k2, p2] to last st, inc. (44 sts)
Row 28: [P2, k2] to end.
Row 29: Inc, p1, [k2, p2] to last 2 sts, k1, inc. (46 sts)
Row 30: K1, [p2, k2] to last st, p1.
Row 31: Inc, [p2, k2] to last st, inc. (48 sts)
Row 32: [K2, p2] to end.
Row 33: Inc, k1, [p2, k2] to last 2 sts, p1, inc. (50 sts)
Row 34: P1, [k2, p2] to last st, k1.
Cont in cl.
Row 35: Inc, [k2,p2] to last st, inc. (52 sts)
Cont in tr.
Row 36: [P2, k2] to end.
Row 37: Inc, p1, [k2, p2] to last 2 sts, k1, inc. (54 sts)
Cast (bind) off.

Neck and Head

Row 1: With tr and RS facing, k7 from spare needle of Right Side of Body, then k7 from spare needle of Left Side of Body. (14 sts)
Row 2: Purl.
Row 3: K2tog, k10, k2tog. (12 sts)
Row 4: Purl.
Row 5: K2tog, k3, [inc] twice, k3, k2tog. (12 sts)
Row 6: Purl.
Rep rows 5–6 twice more.
Cont in ra.
Rep rows 5–6 twice more.
Row 15: K5, k2tog, k5. (11 sts)
Row 16: Purl.
Work 2 rows st st.
Row 19: K9, w&t (leave 2 sts on left-hand needle unworked).
Row 20: Working top of head on centre 7 sts only, p7, w&t.
Row 21: K7, w&t.
Row 22: P7, w&t.
Row 23: K7, w&t.
Row 24: P7, w&t.
Row 25: K7, w&t.
Row 26: P7, w&t.
Row 27: K9. (11 sts in total)
Row 28: P2tog, p7, p2tog. (9 sts)
Row 29: K2tog, p5, k2tog. (7 sts)
Row 30: P2tog, p3, p2tog. (5 sts)
Knit 4 rows.
Row 35: K2tog, k1, k2tog. (3 sts)
Knit 4 rows,
Row 40: K2tog, k1. (2 sts)
Row 41: K2tog and fasten off.

Wing

(make 2 the same)
With ph, cast on 24 sts.
*Row 1: [K2, p2] to end.
Row 2: [K2, p2] to end.
Cont in cl.
Row 3: [K2, p2] to end.
Row 4: [K2, p2] to end.

Wings

It can be difficult to get the turkey to stand up, so bear in mind when you sew on the wings that they need to be fairly far forward to balance the tail.

Cont in ph.*

Rep from * to * twice more.

Row 13: With ph, k2, p2, k2, turn and work on these 6 sts only.

Row 14: P2, k2, p2.

Cont in cl.

Row 15: K2, p2, k2, turn.

Row 16: P2, k2, p2.

Rep rows 13–16, 3 times more.

Cont in ph.

Row 29: K2tog, p2, k2tog. (4 sts)

Row 30: [K2tog] twice. (2 sts)

Row 31: P2tog and fasten off.

Row 32: Rejoin ph to rem sts, **p2, k2, p2, turn and work on these 6 sts only.

Row 33: K2, p2, k2, turn.

Cont in cl.

Row 34: P2, k2, p2, turn.

Row 35: K2, p2, k2.

Cont in ph.**

Rep from ** to ** twice more

Cont in ph.

Row 44: P2tog, k2, p2tog. (4 sts)

Row 45: [P2tog] twice. (2 sts)

Row 46: K2tog and fasten off.

Row 47: Rejoin ph to rem sts and rep rows 13–16 twice more.

Rep rows 29–31 once more.

Rep rows 32–35 once more.

Cont in ph.

Rep rows 44–46 once more.

Wattle

With ra, cast on 5 sts.

Knit 5 rows.

Row 6: K2tog, k1, k2tog. (3 sts)

Knit 15 rows.

Row 22: Inc, k1, inc. (5 sts)

Knit 5 rows.

Cast (bind) off.

Leg and Spur

(make 2 the same)

With cl, cast on 4 sts.

Beg with a k row, work 18 rows st st.

Cast (bind) off.

Outer Claws

(make 2 the same)

With cl, cast on 1 st.

Beg with a k row, cont in st st.

Row 1: Inc. (2 sts)

Row 2: Purl.

Row 3: [Inc] twice. (4 sts)

Work 23 rows st st.

Row 27: [K2tog] twice. (2 sts)

Row 28: Purl.

Row 29: K2tog and fasten off.

Middle Claw

(make 2 the same)

Work as for Outer Claws, but working
11 rows st st.

Cast (bind) off.

Claws

The two outer claws on each foot
are knitted as a single piece, and
the middle claw knitted separately.

To Make Up

SEWING IN ENDS Sew in ends, leaving ends from cast on and cast (bound) off rows for sewing up.

BODY With WS together and whip stitch, sew around the body, leaving a 2.5cm (1in) gap.

HEAD AND BEAK Sew sides of head together, leaving garter stitch beak section (last 10 rows) open flat so that it dangles down.

STUFFING Stuff the turkey firmly, then sew up the gap. Mould body into shape.

LEGS AND FEET Using a 20cm (8in) length of pipecleaner and the Leg and Claw Method (see page 173), make up legs and feet. The turkey's legs are 3cm (1¼in) high. To attach the legs, push protruding ends of pipecleaners into base of body approx 10 rows apart. Strengthen by inserting wooden sticks up backs of legs and into body if necessary.

TAIL Press tail open so that it fans out and sew approx 2.5cm (1in) above bottom of turkey with purl side outwards. Sew up both sides of tail as far as first stripe in cl, then fan out.

WINGS Sew to side of body following angle of chest, approx 3cm (1¼in) down from top chest seam, with long feathers at bottom and short feathers at top.

WATTLE Fold wattle in half and sew centre under chin.

EYES With cd, sew 4 satin stitches on either side of head positioned as in photograph. Sew black beads on centre.

White Rabbit

Prolific breeders, rabbits are well adapted for surviving without help on a farm. They have evolved to fight off predators: they have long ears to aid hearing and strong hind legs for hopping in a zigzag motion; their eyes have a wide field of vision and they sleep with them open; and they live in burrows. Having said all this, they are destructive little creatures, eating their way through our vegetable plot. It's difficult to ascertain why rabbits are kept on farms, but they are charming and symbolic animals, representing fertility and rebirth at Easter.

White Rabbit

With a pom-pom tail, the rabbit is adorable and easy to knit.

Measurements
Length from nose to tail: 13cm (5in)
Height to top of head (excluding ears):
10cm (4in)

Materials
- Pair of 2¾mm (US 2) knitting needles
- Double-pointed 2¾mm (US 2) knitting needles (for holding stitches)
- 10g (¼oz) of Rowan Pure Wool 4ply in Snow 412 (sn)
- 10g (¼oz) of Rowan Kidsilk Haze in Cream 634 (cr)
NOTE: most of this animal uses 1 strand of sn and 1 strand of cr held together, and this is called sncr
- Tiny amount of Rowan Pure Wool 4ply in Shell 468 (sl) for nose and ears
- 2 small pink beads for eyes and sewing needle and pink thread for sewing on
- Nylon thread or fishing line for whiskers
- 1 pipecleaner for front legs

Abbreviations
See page 172.

Right Front Leg
With sncr, cast on 6 sts.
Beg with a k row, work 2 rows st st.
Row 3: Inc, [k2tog] twice, inc. (6 sts)
Work 5 rows st st.
Row 9: Inc, k4, inc. (8 sts)

Body
Knitted in two parts, the rabbit is sewn together along the spine.

Work 3 rows st st.*
Row 13: Cast (bind) off 4 sts, k to end (hold 4 sts on spare needle for Right Side of Body).

Left Front Leg
Work as for Right Front Leg to *.
Row 13: K4, cast (bind) off 4 sts (hold 4 sts on spare needle for Left Side of Body).

Right Side of Body and Head
With sncr, cast on 16 sts.
Beg with a k row, work 4 rows st st.
Row 5: K5, turn and work on these 5 sts only to shape Right Back Leg.
Beg with a p row, work 3 rows st st.
Cast (bind) off.
Row 5: Rejoin yarn to rem 11 sts, k to end.
Row 6: P2, k1, p8, cast on 2 sts. (13 sts)
Row 7: Inc, k1, p1, k7, p1, k2. (14 sts)
Row 8: P2, k1, p6, k1, p3, inc. (15 sts)
Row 9: Inc, k5, p1, k4, p1, k3. (16 sts)
Row 10: P4, k4, p8.
Row 11: Inc, k15. (17 sts)
Row 12: P2tog, p15, with WS facing p4 from spare needle of Right Front Leg. (20 sts)
Row 13: Knit.
Row 14: Purl.
Row 15: Inc, k19. (21 sts)
Row 16: P2tog, p19. (20 sts)
Row 17: Knit.
Row 18: P2tog, p18. (19 sts)
Row 19: Knit.
Row 20: P2tog, p17. (18 sts)
Row 21: Inc, k15, k2tog. (18 sts)
Row 22: P2tog, p16, cast on 3 sts. (20 sts)
Row 23: K18, k2tog. (19 sts)
Row 24: P2tog, p16, inc. (19 sts)
Row 25: K17, k2tog. (18 sts)
Row 26: Cast (bind) off 8 sts, p9 icos, inc. (11 sts)
Row 27: Knit.
Row 28: P9, p2tog. (10 sts)
Row 29: K2tog, k8. (9 sts)
Row 30: P2tog, p5, p2tog. (7 sts)

Front Legs
When attaching tummy to body, make sure the front legs are level.

Tail
Fluff up the pom-pom tail before attaching it.

Row 31: Knit.
Row 32: P5, p2tog. (6 sts)
Cast (bind) off.

Left Side of Body and Head
With sncr, cast on 16 sts.
Beg with a p row, work 4 rows st st.
Row 5: P5, turn and work on these 5 sts only to shape Left Back Leg.
Beg with a k row, work 3 rows st st.
Cast (bind) off.
Row 5: Rejoin yarn to rem 11 sts, p to end.
Row 6: K2, p1, k8, cast on 2 sts. (13 sts)
Row 7: Inc, p1, k1, p7, k1, p2. (14 sts)
Row 8: K2, p1, k6, p1, k3, inc. (15 sts)
Row 9: Inc, p5, k1, p4, k1, p3. (16 sts)
Row 10: K4, p4, k8.
Row 11: Inc, p15. (17 sts)
Row 12: K2tog, k15, with RS facing k4 from spare needle of Left Front Leg. (20 sts)
Row 13: Purl.
Row 14: Knit.
Row 15: Inc, p19. (21 sts)
Row 16: K2tog, k19. (20 sts)
Row 17: Purl.
Row 18: K2tog, k18. (19 sts)
Row 19: Purl.
Row 20: K2tog, k17. (18 sts)
Row 21: Inc, p15, p2tog. (18 sts)
Row 22: K2tog, k16, cast on 3 sts. (20 sts)
Row 23: P18, p2tog. (19 sts)
Row 24: K2tog, k16, inc. (19 sts)
Row 25: P17, p2tog. (18 sts)
Row 26: Cast (bind) off 8 sts, k9 icos, inc. (11 sts)
Row 27: Purl.
Row 28: K9, k2tog. (10 sts)
Row 29: P2tog, p8. (9 sts)
Row 30: K2tog, k5, k2tog. (7 sts)
Row 31: Purl.
Row 32: K5, k2tog. (6 sts)
Cast (bind) off.

Tummy
With sncr, cast on 4 sts.
Beg with a k row, work 42 rows st st.
Row 43: [K2tog] twice. (2 sts)
Work 2 rows st st.
Row 46: P2tog and fasten off.

Ear
(make 2 the same)
With sncr, cast on 4 sts.
Beg with a k row, work 2 rows st st.
Row 3: Inc, k2, inc. (6 sts)
Work 7 rows st st.
Row 11: K2tog, k2, k2tog. (4 sts)
Row 12: Purl.
Row 13: [K2tog] twice. (2 sts)
Row 14: P2tog and fasten off.

Lining of Ear
(make 2 the same)
With sl, cast on 3 sts.
Beg with a k row, work 10 rows st st.
Row 11: K2tog, k1. (2 sts)
Row 12: Purl.
Row 13: K2tog and fasten off.

Tail
With sncr, make a pom-pom.
Cut two 2.5cm (1in) cardboard discs and cut a 1.25cm (½in) hole in the centre of each. Hold the discs together and wind the yarn around the ring as evenly as possible until the hole is almost filled with yarn (it is quicker to wind several strands at once). Then thread the yarn onto a needle and continue to wind until the hole is closed up. Cut the yarn around the edge of the circles. Ease the cardboard discs slightly apart and wrap a long length of doubled yarn between them and around the centre of the pom-pom. Tie the pom-pom together tightly at the centre, leaving the long tail to use for attaching pom-pom to rabbit. Then cut the cardboard away from the pom-pom. Fluff up the pom-pom and trim if necessary.

To Make Up

SEWING IN ENDS Sew in ends, leaving ends from cast on and cast (bound) off rows for sewing up.

LEGS With WS together and whip stitch, fold each leg in half and sew up legs on RS, starting at paws.

BODY Sew around bottom, along body and around head to neck of rabbit.

TUMMY Sew cast on row of tummy to base of rabbit's bottom, and sew cast (bound) off row to neck. Ease and sew tummy to fit body. Leave a 2.5cm (1in) gap between front and back legs on one side.

STUFFING Pipecleaners are used to stiffen the front legs and help bend them into shape. Fold a pipecleaner into a U-shape and measure against front two legs. Cut to fit approximately, leaving an extra 2.5cm (1in) at both ends. Fold these ends over to stop pipecleaner poking out of the paws. Roll a little stuffing around pipecleaner and slip into body, one end down each front leg. Starting at the head, stuff the rabbit firmly, then sew up the gap. Mould body into shape.

TAIL Attach pom-pom to rabbit's bottom.

EARS With WS together, sew ear to lining. Slightly pinch bottom of each ear and sew cast on row to top of head, with lining facing outwards and 2 rows between ears.

EYES Sew on pink beads positioned as in photograph.

NOSE With sl, sew 2 vertical sts followed by 2 horizontal sts in a T-shape at tip of nose.

WHISKERS Cut six 8cm (3in) lengths of fishing line, thread through cheeks and trim.

Sheepdog

Sheepdogs are very bright and need lots of stimulation. They are bred to work and will get bored if they aren't given tasks. In an early scene in Thomas Hardy's *Far from the Madding Crowd*, Gabriel Oak's sheepdog goes rogue and drives his entire flock of sheep over a cliff. *One Man and His Dog*, an amazingly hypnotic and successful television series showing sheepdog trials, originally ran for 30 years and has recently been revived.

Sheepdog

This perky sheepdog is an athletic and working version of our own Border Collie.

Measurements

Length from nose to tail: 21cm (8¼in)
Height to top of head: 11cm (4½in)

Materials

- Pair of 2¾mm (US 2) knitting needles
- Double-pointed 2¾mm (US 2) knitting needles (for tail and for holding stitches)
- 10g (¼oz) of Rowan Kidsilk Haze in Cream 634 (cr) used DOUBLE throughout
- 15g (½oz) of Rowan Pure Wool 4ply in Black 404 (bl)
- 2 pipecleaners for legs and tail
- 2 tiny black beads for eyes and sewing needle and black thread for sewing on

Abbreviations

See page 172.
See page 173 for Loopy Stitch. Work 2-finger loopy stitch throughout pattern.
See page 172 for Wrap and Turn Method.
See page 172 for I-cord Technique.

Right Back Leg

With cr, cast on 7 sts.
Beg with a k row, work 2 rows st st.
Row 3: Inc, k2tog, k1, k2tog, inc. (7 sts)
Work 7 rows st st.*
Join in bl.
Row 11: Inccr, k2cr, k3bl, incbl. (9 sts)
Row 12: P5bl, 4cr.

Row 13: Inccr, k3cr, k4bl, incbl. (11 sts)
Row 14: P6bl, 5cr.
Row 15: Inccr, k4cr, k5bl, incbl. (13 sts)
Row 16: P7bl, 6cr.
Row 17: Inccr, k5cr, k6bl, incbl. (15 sts)
Row 18: P8bl, p7cr.
Row 19: Cast (bind off) 7 sts cr, k1cr icos, k7bl (hold 8 sts on spare needle for Right Side of Body).

Left Back Leg

Work as for Right Back Leg to *.
Join in bl.
Row 11: Inc, k3bl, k2cr, inc. (9 sts)
Row 12: P4cr, p5bl.
Row 13: Incbl, k4bl, k3cr, inccr. (11 sts)

Tummy

The sheepdog has a fluffy tummy made from cut loopy stitches.

Row 14: P5cr, p6bl.
Row 15: Incbl, k5bl, k4cr, inccr. (13 sts)
Row 16: P6cr, p7bl.
Row 17: Incbl, k6bl, k5cr, inccr. (15 sts)
Row 18: P7cr, p8bl.
Row 19: K8bl, cast (bind) off 7 sts cr (hold 8 sts on spare needle for Left Side of Body).

Right Front Leg
With cr, cast on 7 sts.
Work as for Right Back Leg to *.
Row 11: Inc, loopy st 1, k3, loopy st 1, inc. (9 sts)
Row 12: Purl.

Row 13: K1, loopy st 1, k5, loopy st 1, k1.
Row 14: Purl.
Row 15: Inc, loopy st 1, k5, loopy st 1, inc. (11 sts)
Row 16: Purl.
Row 17: Inc, loopy st 1, k7, loopy st 1, inc. (13 sts)
Row 18: Purl.**
Row 19: Cast (bind) off 6 sts, k to end (hold 7 sts on spare needle for Right Side of Body).

Left Front Leg
Work as for Right Front Leg to **.
Row 19: K7, cast (bind) off 6 sts (hold 7 sts on spare needle for Left Side of Body).

Right Side of Body
Row 1: With cr, cast on 1 st, with RS facing k7cr from spare needle of Right Front Leg, with bl cast on 15 sts, k8bl from spare needle of Right Back Leg. (31 sts)
Row 2: P23bl, p8cr.
Row 3: Inccr, k8cr, k22bl. (32 sts)
Row 4: P22bl, p10cr.
Row 5: K9cr, k23bl.
Row 6: P23bl, p9cr.
Row 7: Inccr, k8cr, k23bl. (33 sts)
Row 8: P24bl, p9cr.
Row 9: K9cr, k24bl.
Row 10: P25bl, p8cr.
Row 11: Inccr, k7cr, k25bl. (34 sts)
Row 12: P2togbl, k24bl, p8cr. (33 sts)
Row 13: K7cr, k24bl, k2togbl. (32 sts)
Row 14: P2togbl, p23bl, p7cr. (31 sts)
Row 15: K7cr, k22bl, k2togbl. (30 sts)
Row 16: Cast (bind) off 22 sts bl, p1bl icos, p7cr (hold 8 sts on spare needle for Neck and Head).

Left Side of Body
Row 1: With cr, cast on 1 st, with WS facing p7cr from spare needle of Left Front Leg, with bl cast on 15 sts, p8bl from spare needle of Left Back Leg. (31 sts)

Body
The sheepdog is knitted in a contrasting combination of double mohair and 4ply wool.

Row 2: K23bl, k8cr.
Row 3: Inccr, p8cr, p22bl. (32 sts)
Row 4: K22bl, k10cr.
Row 5: P9cr, p23bl.
Row 6: K23bl, k9cr.
Row 7: Inccr, p8cr, p23bl. (33 sts)
Row 8: K24bl, k9cr.
Row 9: P9cr, p24bl.
Row 10: K25bl, k8cr.
Row 11: Inccr, p7cr, p25bl. (34 sts)
Row 12: K2togbl, k24bl, k8cr. (33 sts)
Row 13: P7cr, p24bl, p2togbl. (32 sts)
Row 14: K2togbl, k23bl, k7cr. (31 sts)
Row 15: P7cr, p22bl, p2togbl. (30 sts)
Row 16: Cast (bind) off 22 sts bl, k1bl icos,
k7cr (hold 8 sts on spare needle for Neck
and Head).

Neck and Head

Row 1: With cr and RS facing, k8 from spare
needle of Right Side of Body, then k8 from
spare needle of Left Side of Body. (16 sts)
Row 2: Purl.
Row 3: Knit.
Row 4: P7, p2tog, p7. (15 sts)
Join in bl.
Row 5: K4bl, k7cr, k4bl.
Row 6: P4bl, p7cr, p4bl.
Row 7: K5bl, k5cr, k2bl, w&t (leave 3 sts on
right-hand needle unworked).
Row 8: Working top of head on centre 9 sts
only, p2bl, p5cr, p2bl, w&t.
Row 9: K2bl, k5cr, k2bl, w&t.
Row 10: P2bl, p5cr, p2bl, w&t.
Row 11: K2bl, k5cr, k5bl. (15 sts in total)
Row 12: P6bl, p3cr, p6bl.
Row 13: K6bl, k3cr, k2bl, w&t (leave 4 sts on
right-hand needle unworked).
Row 14: Working top of head on centre 7 sts
only, p2bl, p3cr, p2bl, w&t.
Row 15: K2bl, k3cr, k2bl, w&t.
Row 16: P2bl, p3cr, p2bl, w&t.
Row 17: K2bl, k3cr, k6bl. (15 sts in total)
Row 18: P4bl, p2togbl, p3cr, p2togbl, p4bl.

(13 sts)
Row 19: K4bl, k5cr, k4bl.
Cont in cr.
Row 20: Purl.
Row 21: K3, k2tog, k3, k2tog, k3. (11 sts)
Work 3 rows st st.
Row 25: K2, k2tog, k3, k2tog, k2. (9 sts)
Work 3 rows st st.
Cast (bind) off.

Tummy

With cr, cast on 1 st.
Beg with a p row, cont in st st.
Row 1: Inc. (2 sts)
Row 2: [Inc] twice. (4 sts)
Row 3: Purl.
Row 4: Inc, k2, inc. (6 sts)
Work 9 rows st st.
Row 14: K1, loopy st 1, k2, loopy st 1, k1.
Row 15: Purl.
Work 2 rows st st.
Rep last 4 rows 4 times more.
Work 30 rows st st.
Row 64: K2tog, k2, k2tog. (4 sts)
Work 9 rows st st.
Cast (bind) off.

Tail

With double-pointed needles and bl, cast
on 7 sts.
Work i-cord as folls:
Knit 7 rows.
Row 8: K2tog, k3, k2tog. (5 sts)
Row 9: K1, loopy st 1, k1, loopy st 1, k1.
Row 10: Knit.
Rep rows 9–10, 4 times more.
Change to cr.
Row 19: K1, loopy st 1, k1, loopy st 1, k1.
Row 20: Knit.
Row 21: K1, loopy st 1, k1, loopy st 1, k1.
Row 22: Knit.
Row 23: K2tog, loopy st 1, k2tog. (3 sts)
Row 24: Purl.
Row 25: K3tog and fasten off.

Tail

The sheepdog's tail is cut loopy
stitch with a white tip.

Ear

(make 2 the same)
With bl, cast on 5 sts.
Beg with a k row, work 2 rows st st.
Knit 5 rows.
Row 8: K2tog, k1, k2tog. (3 sts)
Row 9: K3tog and fasten off.

To Make Up

SEWING IN ENDS Sew in ends, leaving ends from cast on and cast (bound) off rows for sewing up.

LEGS With WS together and whip stitch, fold each leg in half and sew up legs on RS, starting at paws.

BODY Sew along back of sheepdog and 2.5cm (1in) down bottom.

TUMMY Sew cast on row of tummy to where you have finished sewing down bottom, and sew cast (bound) off row to nose. Ease and sew tummy to fit body. Leave a 2.5cm (1in) gap between front and back legs on one side.

STUFFING Pipecleaners are used to stiffen the legs and help bend them into shape. Fold a pipecleaner into a U-shape and measure against front two legs. Cut to fit approximately, leaving an extra 2.5cm (1in) at both ends. Fold these ends over to stop the pipecleaner poking out of the paws. Roll a little stuffing around pipecleaner and slip into body, one end down each front leg. Repeat with second pipecleaner and back legs. Starting at the head, stuff the sheepdog firmly, then sew up the gap. Mould body into shape. Cut and trim loops.

TAIL Cut a 5cm (2in) length of leftover pipecleaner and insert into cast on end of tail with approx 3cm (1¼in) of pipecleaner sticking out. Push protruding end of pipecleaner into dog's body at start of bottom. With loops on underside, attach cast on row of tail to bottom and bend tail into shape. Cut and trim loops.

EARS Sew cast on row of each ear to top of head approx 5 rows back from where black patches end at front of face, with 4 sts between ears.

EYES With bl, sew 2-loop French knots positioned as in photograph, 1 st down from where black ends with 3 sts between eyes. Sew black beads on top of knots.

NOSE With bl, sew 3 satin stitches horizontally across tip of nose.

Hints

Choosing Yarns

We recommend Rowan Yarns, but as each animal takes only a small amount of yarn, any yarn can be used, either different colours or thicknesses. If using thicker yarns, refer to the ball band for needle size, but use needles that are at least two sizes smaller than recommended as the tension (gauge) needs to be tight so the stuffing doesn't show. If using thicker yarn and larger needles, your animal will be considerably bigger. We feel that finer yarns create a more refined animal.

Knitting the Body and Head

When holding stitches to use later on in the pattern, eg on the final row of the legs, work the last row on a spare double-pointed needle. This means you can pick up and knit or purl the stitches from either end of the needle.

After you have sewn up the back of the animal, there may be a hole at the nape of the neck. Work a couple of Swiss darning stitches to fill the hole.

Carefully follow the instructions when picking up and knitting the first row of Neck and Head. The right side of the body is knitted first, then the left side. The backbone of the animal is in the middle of this row. If picked up incorrectly the head will be facing towards the tail.

Holes can develop around the short-row shaping at the top of the head. When sewing on the ears, use the sewing-up end to patch up any holes. Swiss darning can also be used to cover up any untidy stitches.

Stuffing the Animal

Stuffing the animal is as important as the actual knitting.

Use a knitting needle point to push the stuffing into the feet, and into the nose of the animal. Even after the animal is sewn up you can manipulate the stuffing with a knitting needle. If the stitches are distorted you have overstuffed your animal.

We recommend using 100% polyester or kapok stuffing, which is available from craft shops and online retailers. An animal takes 20–60g (¾–2¼oz) of stuffing depending on size.

An Important Note

The animals aren't toys, but if you intend to give them to small children do not use pipecleaners in the construction. Instead, you will need to densely stuff the legs to make the animal stand up.

Unfortunately, for some animals the pipecleaners are essential to sculpt some of their unique features – for instance, the horns of the ram.

Methods

Abbreviations

alt alternate
approx approximately
beg begin(ning)
cm centimetres
cont continue
foll(s) follow(s)(ing)
g grams
icos including cast (bound) off stitch. After casting (binding) off the stated number of stitches, one stitch remains on the right-hand needle. This stitch is included in the number of the following group of stitches.
in inches
inc work into front and back of next stitch to increase by one stitch
k knit
k2(3)tog knit next two (three) stitches together
oz ounces
p purl
p2(3)tog purl next two (three) stitches together
rem remain(ing)
rep repeat
rev reverse
RS right side
st(s) stitch(es)
st st stocking (stockinette) stitch
w&t wrap and turn. See Wrap and Turn Method, right.
WS wrong side
[ ] work instructions within square brackets as directed
* work instructions after asterisk(s) as directed

Colour Knitting

There are two main techniques for working with more than one colour in the same row of knitting: the intarsia technique and the Fair Isle technique.

Intarsia Technique
This method is used when knitting individual, large blocks of colour. It is best to use a small ball (or long length) for each area of colour, otherwise the yarns will easily become tangled. When changing to a new colour, twist the yarns on the wrong side of the work to prevent holes forming. When starting a new row, turn the knitting so that the yarns that are hanging from it untwist as much as possible. If you have several colours you may occasionally have to reorganize the yarns at the back of the knitting. Your work may look messy, but once the ends are all sewn in it will look fine.

Fair Isle (or Stranding) Technique
If there are no more than four stitches between colours you can use the Fair Isle technique. Begin knitting with the first colour, then drop this when you introduce the second colour. When you come to the first colour again, take it under the second colour to twist the yarns. When you come to the second colour again, take it over the first colour. The secret is not to pull the strands on the wrong side of the work too tightly or the work will pucker.

I-cord Technique

With double-pointed needles, *knit a row. Slide the stitches to the other end of the needle. Do not turn the knitting. Repeat from *, pulling the yarn tight on the first stitch so that the knitting forms a tube.

Wrap and Turn Method (w&t)

Knit the number of stitches in the first short row. Slip the next stitch purlwise from the left-hand to the right-hand needle. Bring the yarn forward then slip the stitch back onto the left-hand needle. Return the yarn to the back. On a purl row use the same method, taking the yarn back then forward.

Short Row Patterning

This is worked by wrapping the stitch as for Wrap and Turn (above), but the number of stitches worked is decreased by one for as many rows as given in the pattern, then increased to the original number of stitches.

Bobble Method

Bobbles are used to make teats on the cow's udders. Work a 3-stitch bobble as follows: knit into the front and back of the stitch once, then knit into the front again, turn. Working on these 3 stitches and beginning with a purl row, work 4 rows st st. Using the left-hand needle, lift the second and third stitches in turn over the first stitch and off the needle. Continue knitting to the position of the next bobble.

Loopy Stitch

On a knit row, knit one stitch as normal, but leave the stitch on the left-hand needle. Bring the yarn from the back to the front between the two needles. Loop the yarn around the fingers of your left hand; the number of fingers needed is specified in each pattern. Take the yarn back between the two needles to the back of the work. Knit the stitch from the left-hand needle as normal. You now have two stitches on the right-hand needle and a loop between them. Pass the first stitch over the second stitch to trap the loop, which is now secure. The end of the loop can be cut when finishing the animal.

As a guide, a 2-finger loop should be about 3–4cm (1¼–1½in) long and a 3-finger loop 6cm (2½in).

Scarf Fringe Method

Use this method for adding tassels to manes and tails. Cut the required lengths of yarn and fold in half, as specified in the pattern. Slip a crochet hook through a knitted stitch, hook the folded end of yarn through the stitch, slip the ends through the loop and pull the yarn tightly. Once all fringing has been done, trim to the required length.

Leg and Claw Method

Cockerel and turkey

Cut a length of pipecleaner 1.5cm (½in) longer than the Leg and Spur and wrap the knitting around it, leaving 1.5cm (½in) of pipecleaner protruding to attach to the bird's body. Sew up using whip stitch. Cut a length of pipecleaner to fit the Outer Claws and another to fit the Middle Claw, and sew up knitting around them as before.

Bend bottom 1.5cm (½in) of leg to form spur. Bend Outer Claws in the middle at a 45-degree angle and attach with whip stitch to where leg bends to form spur. Sew cast (bound) off row of Middle Claw to centre of bend in Outer Claws.

Hen, chick and silkie

Measure along pipecleaner the length of the bird's leg plus 1.5cm (½in) for attaching the leg to the body. Bend at a right angle to form the joint between leg and foot.

Working with the long end of the pipecleaner, measure 1.5cm (½in) along it and then fold it back on itself and twist it around the bottom of the leg to form the first front claw. Make the second front claw in the same way, fully twisting the folded-back pipecleaner around the bottom of the leg. Repeat to make the back claw to form a tripod-shaped foot. Twist the excess pipecleaner up the leg to secure and cut off any surplus.

Wrap the shorter piece of knitting around the back and second claws and sew up using whip stitch. Sew up the longer piece of knitting around the leg and first front claw.

Wrapping Pipecleaners in Yarn

This method is used for very thin legs and for claws: if possible, use coloured pipecleaners and try to match the colour of the wrapping yarn. Leaving a 5cm (2in) tail of free yarn, tightly wrap the yarn around the pipecleaner, making sure no pipecleaner chenille pokes through. Continue wrapping down the pipecleaner to as close to the tip as possible, then wrap the yarn back up to the top of the pipecleaner. Knot the two ends and slip them into the body. If there is a little bit of white pipecleaner chenille showing, colour it in with a matching felt-tip pen. A little dab of clear glue will stop the wrapping from slipping off the end of the pipecleaner.

Index of Animals

8

14

22

28

34

40

46

54

60

66

72

78

86

92

98

104

112

118

126

132

138

144

150

158

164

Resources

All the animals are knitted in Rowan Yarns; for stockists please refer to the Rowan website: www.knitrowan.com. By the time this book is printed some colours may have been discontinued; John Lewis department stores stock Rowan yarns, and will happily suggest alternative colours.

We are selling knitting kits for some of the farm animals. The kits are packaged in a knitting bag and contain yarn, all needles required, stuffing, pipecleaners and a pattern.

For those who cannot knit but would like a farm animal, we are selling some of the animals ready-made. You can see the farm animals on our website: www.muirandosborne.co.uk.

The Authors

Sally Muir and Joanna Osborne run their own knitwear business, Muir and Osborne. They export their knitwear to stores in the United States, Japan and Europe as well as selling to shops in the United Kingdom. Several pieces of their knitwear are in the permanent collection at the Victoria and Albert Museum, London. They are the authors of the bestselling *Best in Show: Knit Your Own Dog*, *Best in Show: 25 More Dogs to Knit* and *Best in Show: Knit Your Own Cat*.

Acknowledgements

Yet again we have had the same lovely team working on this book, so thank you to Katie Cowan, Amy Christian and Laura Russell at Pavilion Books, Carolyn Dawnay and Sophie Scard at United Agents and Marilyn Wilson, Kate Haxell and Michelle Pickering for their excellent work on the patterns. Thank you to Holly for an even more gorgeous set of photographs, and the National Trust at Saddlescombe Farm for letting us use their beautiful buildings and surroundings for the photographs and, once again, thank you so much to Rowan for their generosity with the yarns.

Join our online community at
www.bestinshowbooks.com